The Journal of Andrew Fuller Studies

Published in the United States of America by
by The Andrew Fuller Center for Baptist Studies
The Southern Baptist Theological Seminary
2825 Lexington Road
Louisville, Kentucky 40280

© The Andrew Fuller Center for Baptist Studies 2020

All rights reserved. No part of this publication may be reproduced, stored in a retrieval system, or transmitted, in any form or by any means, without the prior permission in writing of The Andrew Fuller Center for Baptist Studies, or as expressly permitted by law, by license, or under terms agreed with the appropriate reproduction rights organization.

ISBN 978-1-989174-70-8

Printed by H&E Publishing, Peterborough, Ontario, Canada

The Journal for Andrew Fuller Studies

The *Journal of Andrew Fuller Studies* is an open access, double-blind peer-reviewed, scholarly journal published online biannually in February and September by the Andrew Fuller Center for Baptist Studies (under the auspices of The Southern Baptist Theological Seminary). The publication language of the journal is English. Articles that deal with the life, ministry, and thought of the Baptist pastor-theologian Andrew Fuller are very welcome, as well as essays on his friends, his Particular Baptist community in the long eighteenth century (1680s–1830s), and the global impact of his thought, known as "Fullerism."

Articles and book reviews are to follow generally the style of Kate L. Turabian, *A Manual for Writers of Research Papers, Theses, and Dissertations*, 9th ed. (Chicago: University of Chicago Press, 2018). They may be submitted in British, American, Australian, New Zealand, or Canadian English. Articles should be between 5,000 and 8,000 words, excluding footnotes. Articles are to be sent to the Editor and book reviews to the Book Review Editors.

Editor: Michael A G Haykin, FRHistS
Chair & Professor of Church History
& Director, The Andrew Fuller Center for Baptist Studies
The Southern Baptist Theological Seminary, Louisville, Kentucky
mhaykin@sbts.edu

Associate editors: Ian Hugh Clary, PhD
Assistant Professor of Historical Theology
Colorado Christian University, Lakewood, Colorado
iclary@ccu.edu

Baiyu Andrew Song, PhD cand.
The Southern Baptist Theological Seminary
Louisville, Kentucky
& Part-time lecturer, Redeemer University, Ancaster, Ontario
bsong677@students.sbts.edu

Design editor: Dustin W. Benge, PhD
Provost & Professor in Church History
Union School of Theology, Bridgend, Wales

Book review editors: Josiah Michael Claassen, PhD cand.
The Southern Baptist Theological Seminary, Louisville, Kentucky
jclaassen800@students.sbts.edu

C. Anthony Neel, PhD cand.
The Southern Baptist Theological Seminary, Louisville, Kentucky
cneel914@students.sbts.edu

Editorial board
Cindy Aalders, DPhil
Director of the John Richard Allison Library
Assistant Professor of the History of Christianity
Regent College, Vancouver

Dustin W. Benge, PhD
Provost & Professor in Church History
Union School of Theology, Bridgend, Wales

Dustin B. Bruce, PhD
Dean & Assistant Professor of Christian Theology and Church History
Boyce College, Louisville, Kentucky

Chris W. Crocker, PhD
Pastor, Markdale Baptist Church, ON
Associate Professor of Church History,
Toronto Baptist Seminary, Ontario

Chris Chun, PhD
Professor of Church History & Director of the *Jonathan Edwards Center*
Gateway Seminary, Ontario, California

Jenny-Lyn de Klerk, PhD cand.,
Midwestern Baptist Theological Seminary,
Kansas City, MO
& Puritan Project Assistant
Regent College, Vancouver

Jason G. Duesing, PhD
Provost & Professor of Historical Theology
Midwestern Baptist Theological Seminary, Kansas City, Missouri

Nathan A. Finn, PhD
Provost & Dean of the University Faculty
North Greenville University, Tigerville, South Carolina

C. Ryan Griffith, PhD
Independent scholar, Minneapolis, Minnesota

Peter Morden, PhD
Senior Pastor/Team Leader, Cornerstone Baptist Church
Leeds, England
& Distinguished Visiting Scholar
Spurgeon's College, London

Adriaan C. Neele, PhD
Director, Doctoral Program
& Professor of Historical Theology
Puritan Reformed Theological Seminary, Grand Rapids, Michigan
& Research Scholar
Yale University, Jonathan Edwards Center, New Haven, Connecticut

Tom Nettles, PhD
Senior Professor of Historical Theology
The Southern Baptist Theological Seminary, Louisville, Kentucky

Robert Strivens, PhD
Pastor, Bradford on Avon Baptist Church (UK)
& Lecturer in Church History, London Seminary

S. Blair Waddell, PhD
Pastor, Providence Baptist Church, Huntsville, Alabama
& Lecturer in Communications, Church History, & New Testament
The Birmingham Theological Seminary Birmingham, Alabama

Steve Weaver, PhD
Pastor, Farmdale Baptist Church
Frankfort, Kentucky
& Adjunct Professor of Church History
The Southern Baptist Theological Seminary, Louisville, Kentucky

Contents

The Journal of Andrew Fuller Studies
No. 1, September 2020

Editorial   9
Michael A.G. Haykin

Articles
John Gill and the charge of hyper-Calvinism: 11
Assessing contemporary arguments in defense
of Gill in light of Gill's doctrine of eternal justification
David Mark Rathel

"Be reconciled to trying disciplines":   31
Andrew Fuller's pastorate at Soham, 1775–1782
Peter J. Morden

"The poisonous influence of a corrupt   47
Antinomian leaven": Caleb Evans' response
to the Antinomianism of William Huntington
Casey G. McCall

Texts & documents
Extracts from six letters written by   59
Benjamin Beddome in 1759 and 1760
ed. and annotated Gary Brady

On being missional—a letter of Andrew Fuller   67
to George Charles Smith
ed. Michael A.G. Haykin

"A juster idea of character": Robert Hall, Jr.   73
on the competing biographies of Andrew Fuller
by J.W. Morris and John Ryland, Jr.
introd. and ed. C. Ryan Griffith

Book Reviews   83

Editorial

Michael A.G. Haykin

Michael A.G. Haykin is Chair and Professor of Church History and Director, The Andrew Fuller Center for Baptist Studies at The Southern Baptist Theological Seminary, Louisville, Kentucky.

The Journal of Andrew Fuller Studies is designed to provide academic reflection on the life and thought of Andrew Fuller, who, nearly seventy-five years ago, was described by A.C. Underwood as "the soundest and most creatively useful theologian the Particular Baptists have ever had."[1] For much of the twentieth century, though, little attention was paid to Fuller. Though there were a small number of articles and a few academic theses on him, Gilbert S. Laws' popular biography, *Andrew Fuller: Pastor, Theologian, Ropeholder*, was the only book focused on Fuller that was published in this entire century.[2] In the past two decades, though, Fuller's "extraordinary importance in the history of theology"—to quote the words of British Baptist historian David Bebbington[3]—has been increasingly recognized. This journal seeks to be a channel for this renaissance of Fuller studies.[4]

Articles will deal with Fuller's life and thought as well as the key roles that Fuller, his circle of friends, and his theological perspective—known as "Fullerism" while he was still alive—played in both the revitalization of the Brit-

---

[1] A. C. Underwood, *A History of the English Baptists* (London: The Baptist Union Publication Dept. [Kingsgate Press], 1947), 166.

[2] Gilbert S. Laws, *Andrew Fuller: Pastor, Theologian, Ropeholder* (London: Carey Press, 1942).

[3] David Bebbington, e-mail to Michael A.G. Haykin, March 11, 2009.

[4] See Nathan A. Finn, "The Renaissance in Andrew Fuller Studies: A Bibliographic Essay," *The Southern Baptist Journal of Theology*, 17, no.2 (Summer 2013): 44–61.

ish Baptists as well as in the launching of the modern missionary movement. Papers that focus on the history of the Particular Baptists in the long eighteenth century—the ecclesial community that was the scene of Fuller's life and thought—will also have a place in this journal as well as essays that deal with the various aspects of the direct impact of Fullerism in the Anglo-American world of Evangelicalism. Each issue will also feature a few critically-edited primary sources, either newly-discovered texts or long-forgotten documents, as well as book reviews relevant to the main concerns of the journal.

May the triune God, who was loved and served by Andrew Fuller, ultimately bless this academic endeavour for the edification of his people and the glorification of his divine Name.

John Gill and the charge of hyper-Calvinism: assessing contemporary arguments in defense of Gill in light of Gill's doctrine of eternal justification

David Mark Rathel

David Rathel received his PhD in Divinity from the University of St Andrews in Scotland and currently serves as Associate Professor of Christian Theology at Gateway Seminary.

For Baptists, John Gill (1697–1771) has great historical significance.[1] He pastored a church meeting at Goat Yard, Horsleydown, in Southwark, London, and this meeting later became the Metropolitan Tabernacle famously led by Charles Spurgeon. Gill was the first Baptist to write a commentary on every book of the Bible and the first Baptist to compose a comprehensive systematic theology. Both his pastoral work and extensive writing ministry allowed him to exercise considerable influence among Particular Baptists during the eighteenth century.[2]

Though recognizing Gill's importance, historians disagree over the nature

---

[1] This article is an expanded version of David Mark Rathel, "Was John Gill a Hyper-Calvinist?: Determining Gill's Theological Identity," *Baptist Quarterly* 48, no. 1 (2017): 47–59. I express here my gratitude to the editors of *Baptist Quarterly* and to Taylor and Francis Publishing for their willingness to have it republished and to Michael A. G. Haykin for accepting it in *The Journal of Andrew Fuller Studies*. I also express appreciation to Stephen R. Holmes, my doctoral supervisor, for his feedback during the construction of this paper.

[2] For a brief introduction to Gill's ministry and influence, consider Timothy George, "John Gill," in *Theologians of the Baptist Tradition*, ed. Timothy George and David Dockery (Nashville, TN: Broadman & Holman, 2001), 11–33.

of his theology. Some consider him a hyper-Calvinist who did not offer the Gospel freely and who denied duty faith, that is, the belief that all sinners have a duty to respond positively to the Gospel. Others defend him from this charge and present him as a model evangelical pastor.[3] Debate over Gill's theology remains an important issue in the study of Baptist history.[4] Much of this disagreement originates from the fact that historians have rarely examined Gill on his own terms. Arguments that portray him as a hyper-Calvinist rely often on guilt by association, incorrect claims about his theological convictions, or preconceived understandings of what constitutes genuine Calvinism.[5] As I will demonstrate, arguments offered in defense of Gill fare little better. They often fail to interpret Gill's soteriology accurately.

Students of Baptist history should seek to discern Gill's true theological identity by carefully examining his theological convictions. I aim to contribute to this cause by surveying his primary theological focus—a desire to minimize human agency in the reception of salvation—and its chief accompanying

---

[3] The most significant work yet published on Gill illustrates this disagreement; it contains articles by respected Gill interpreters who argue for both readings. See Michael A.G. Haykin, ed., *The Life and Thought of John Gill (1697–1771): A Tercentennial Appreciation* (Leiden/New York/Köln: Brill, 1997). The phrase hyper-Calvinist is not one without ambiguity, but it often appears in the literature related to Gill to describe his alleged denial of Gospel offers and duty faith. I employ it here for this reason.

[4] See, for example, George M. Ella, "John Gill and the Charge of Hyper-Calvinism," *Baptist Quarterly* 36, no. 4 (1995): 160–170.

[5] Though offering an interesting account of the development of hyper-Calvinism, Peter Toon associates Gill with hyper-Calvinism primarily because of Gill's personal relationships with hyper-Calvinist leaders, not his theology. Peter Toon, *The Emergence of Hyper-Calvinism in English Nonconformity, 1689–1765* (1967, Eugene, OR: Wipf & Stock, 2011), 96–100. Many surveys of Baptist history connect Gill with hyper-Calvinism due to an alleged supralapsarianism. See, for example, J.M. Cramp, *Baptist History* (London: Elliot Stock, 1868), 477; Henry C. Vedder, *A Short History of the Baptists* (Valley Forge, PA: Judson, 1907), 239–241; A.C. Underwood, *A History of the English Baptists* (London: Baptist Union, 1947), 134–135; H. Leon McBeth, *The Baptist Heritage: Four Centuries of Baptist Witness* (Nashville, TN: Broadman & Holman, 1987), 177–178. This assessment is not correct; Gill was not a staunch supralapsarian. See John Gill, *A Complete Body of Doctrinal and Practical Divinity*, new ed. (London: Tegg & Company, 1839), 1:261–265; idem, *A Collection of Sermons and Tracts* (London: George Keith, 1778), 2:73. Curt Daniel, author of the most extensive research on Gill thus far, correctly interprets much of Gill's thought, but he determines that Gill was a hyper-Calvinist in part because of a contrast Daniel draws between Gill and Calvin. See his "Hyper-Calvinism and John Gill" (PhD diss., The University of Edinburgh, 1983), x, 1–40. Not all have found Daniel's approach convincing. See Hong-Gyu Park, "Grace and Nature in John Gill (1697–1771)" (PhD diss., The University of Aberdeen, 2001), 286–287; Richard A. Muller, "John Gill and the Reformed Tradition: A Study in the Reception of Protestant Orthodoxy in the Eighteenth-Century" in Haykin, ed., *The Life and Thought of John Gill*, 52.

doctrine, eternal justification.⁶ I will then probe how Gill's soteriology affected his understanding of Gospel offers and duty faith. I will conclude by interacting with Gill's primary defenders, demonstrating how a failure to read his soteriology correctly has often led to inaccurate portrayals of his true convictions. This approach will reveal that Gill indeed denied Gospel offers and duty faith. Put another way, it connects Gill with a theology that many label hyper-Calvinism.

Eternal justification
The time in which Gill ministered, often labeled the Age of Reason, witnessed considerable theological upheavals, and Gill was, overall, troubled by these changes. He believed that the era's strong commitment to rationalism created theologies that deemphasized the necessity of divine grace. The popularity of such theologies—most notably various forms of Deism and the theology of Daniel Whitby (1638–1726)—pushed him into a defensive position.⁷

Gill responded by creating a theology that sought to magnify divine grace. He feared any position that resembled synergism, and he constructed a theological system that took "the entire economy of salvation up into eternity" and "rendered it impervious to the will of the creature."⁸ Such a move provided Gill a way to speak of salvation in a manner that allowed for minimal human participation.

In Gill's system, election creates an eternal union between the elect and God. Gill believed that just as election "flows from the love of God" eternally, so "there must of course be an union to Him so early." Eternal union is therefore an "eternal immanent act in God" in which there is "the going forth of his heart

---

⁶ Many convictions contributed to Gill's final soteriological position. I choose to highlight eternal justification here because Gill often emphasized it and because it played an important role in shaping his understanding of evangelism. For works that highlight the significance of Gill's doctrine of eternal justification, see Michael A.G. Haykin, "Remembering Baptist Heroes: The Example of John Gill," in *Ministry By His Grace and For His Glory: Essays in Honor of Thomas J. Nettles*, ed. Thomas K. Ascol and Nathan A. Finn (Cape Coral, FL: Founders Press, 2011), 17–37; R. Philip Roberts, *Continuity and Change: London Calvinistic Baptists and the Evangelical Revival, 1760–1820* (Wheaton, IL: Richard Owen Roberts, 1989), 40–41; Alan P.F. Sell, *The Great Debate: Calvinism, Arminianism and Salvation* (1982, Eugene, OR: Wipf & Stock, 1998), 85; Peter Naylor, *Picking Up a Pin for the Lord: English Particular Baptists from 1688 to the Early Nineteenth Century* (London: Grace, 1992), 150.

⁷ For a survey of the Deism's influence during Gill's time, see Alan P.F. Sell, *Enlightenment, Ecumenism, Evangel: Theological Themes and Thinkers, 1550–2000* (Milton Keynes: Paternoster, 2005), 112–131. Gill famously argued against Whitby in John Gill, *The Cause of God and Truth*, new ed. (London: Thomas Tegg and Son, 1838).

⁸ Richard A. Muller, "The Spirit and the Covenant: John Gill's Critique of the *Pactum Salutis*," *Foundations* 24, no. 1 (1981): 12.

in love to them [i.e., the elect], thereby uniting them to himself."⁹

Such a union is possible because election creates for the elect an eternal "being in Christ, a kind of subsistence in him." This is not an actual being, an *esse actu,* but a representative being, an *esse representativum.* Through this representation, the elect "are capable of having grants of grace made to them in Christ." Gill cited texts such as 2 Timothy 1:9 and Ephesians 1:3 to support his position. He noted that such verses claim the elect are "blessed with all spiritual blessings in him, and that before the world began" and contended that the reception of such spiritual blessings requires an eternal union between the elect and Christ.¹⁰

The *pactum salutis* explains how the elect are able to receive these spiritual blessings in this eternal union. In an agreement between the members of the Trinity, the Son promised to serve as surety for the elect; that is, he pledged to atone for their sins at the time of the Father's choosing. The Son's promise to do so was so secure that the Father applied the benefits of the atonement to the elect within the eternal union, before Christ's actual death on the cross.¹¹

Gill highlighted two particular spiritual blessings the elect receive in this union—eternal adoption and eternal justification. Of these, eternal justification received the majority of his attention. He claimed that it is

> an immanent act in God, it is an act of his grace towards them [i.e., the elect], is wholly without them, entirely resides in the divine mind, and lies in his estimating, accounting, and constituting them righteous, through the righteousness of his Son; and, as such, did not first commence in time, but from eternity.¹²

Therefore, for Gill, justification begins not at the moment a person exercises faith or even at the moment of Christ's death on the cross. It is an immanent

---

⁹ Gill, *Complete Body,* 1:284–285. See also Gill's explanation of the connection between unconditional election and eternal justification in one of his earliest works, a sermon on Acts 13:39 published under the title *The Doctrine of Justification* in Gill, *Collection of Sermons and Tracts,* 3:167ff.

¹⁰ Gill, *Complete Body,* 1:286. One wishes that Gill had further clarified his statements about the elect possessing an eternal subsistence in Christ. Unfortunately, he did not do so. One can find other remarks on this subject in Gill, *Collection of Sermons and Tracts,* 2:88; 3:168.

¹¹ See Gill, *Complete Body,* 1:293. For work on Gill's doctrine of the *pactum salutis,* see David Mark Rathel, "Innovating the Covenant of Redemption: John Gill and the History of Redemption as Mere Shadow" (Paper presented at the Annual Meeting of the Evangelical Theological Society, San Antonio, Texas, November 15, 2016).

¹² Gill, *Complete Body,* 1:292. For a helpful exposition of Gill's theology of eternal justification, consider Oliver D. Crisp, *Deviant Calvinism: Broadening Reformed Theology* (Minneapolis, MN: Fortress Press, 2014), 41–70.

and eternal act of God.

Though the elect are justified from eternity, before their faith in Christ and their conversion they are unaware of their justification. For this reason, Gill made a distinction between active justification and passive justification. Active justification, or justification *in foro Dei*, is "strictly and properly justification." It is eternal justification, justification as an immanent and eternal act of God. Passive justification, or justification *in foro conscientiæ*, is "declarative to and upon the conscience of the believer."[13] It occurs in time. Active justification is therefore what one should consider true justification; it is God's declaration that the elect are righteous in his sight. Passive justification, on the other hand, is merely one's personal recognition that one has been eternally justified.

In this scheme, active justification is the form of justification that precedes conversion and regeneration in the *ordo salutis*. It also precedes faith. God justifies the elect from eternity, and this fact is true regardless of whether the elect have yet to place their faith in Christ's atoning work. Gill wrote, "Faith adds nothing to the *esse*, only to the *bene esse* of justification; it is no part of, nor any ingredient in it; it is a complete act in the eternal mind of God, without the being or consideration of faith."[14] Admitting that some biblical texts appear to place faith prior to justification in the *ordo salutis*, he explained, "What scriptures may be thought to speak of faith, as a prerequisite to justification, cannot be understood as speaking of it as a prerequisite to the being of justification; for faith has no causal influence upon it, it adds nothing to its being, it is no ingredient in it, it is not the cause nor matter of it."[15]

Only in relation to passive justification, the *bene esse* of one's justification, does faith have relevance. Texts that connect faith and justification "can only be understood as speaking of faith as a prerequisite to the knowledge and comfort of it."[16] Faith in Christ is therefore only necessary to obtain the assurance that one is justified; it is not necessary for one's actual justification.

While presenting justification in such a manner is unconventional, Gill personally saw great value in his position. Primarily, he believed that it preserved sovereign grace by completely divorcing justification from human effort. The elect do not exercise faith to receive justification; God simply declares them justified through their eternal union with Christ. Gill remarked, "Justification is an act of God's grace towards us, *is wholly without us*, entirely resides in the divine mind, and lies in his estimation, accounting and consti-

---

[13] This statement appears in *The Doctrine of Justification*. See Gill, *Collection of Sermons and Tracts*, 3:150.

[14] Gill, *Complete Body*, 1:293.

[15] Gill, *Complete Body*, 1:298.

[16] Gill, *Complete Body*, 1:298.

tuting us righteous."[17]

Gill even delighted in the fact that his position upended a more traditional understanding of justification by faith. He used harsh language to describe the traditional position, fearing that it would lead to the synergistic forms of salvation that he so often combatted. In a defense of eternal justification and eternal union presented to Abraham Taylor (fl. 1727–1740), he registered his disagreement with theologians who espoused the traditional perspective and questioned why they would hold to such a position. He wrote:

> It is generally said that they [the elect] are not united to Christ until they believe, and that the bond of union is the Spirit on Christ's part, and faith on ours. I am ready to think that these phrases are taken up by divines, one from another, without a thorough consideration of them … Why must this union be pieced up with faith on our part? This smells so prodigious rank of self, that one may justly suspect that something rotten and nauseous lies at the bottom of it.[18]

He followed this statement with a lengthy argument that sought to overturn the traditional understanding of justification by faith.[19]

Gospel offers and duty faith
Gill was a systematic theologian who operated in the style of the seventeenth-century Protestant scholastic theologians he admired, and as such he desired a coherent theological system.[20] His desire for doctrinal consistency led him to shape his understanding of evangelism in accordance with his convictions about eternal justification. Here in his thought, one finds strong denials of Gospel offers and duty faith. Concerning the offer of the Gospel, Gill argued:

> The gospel is not tendered to the elect, but is *the power of God unto salvation* to them. The grace of God is bestowed upon them, applied to them,

---

[17] This statement appears in *The Doctrine of Justification*. See Gill, *Collection of Sermons and Tracts*, 3:167. Italics added.

[18] This statement appears in Gill's tract entitled *The Doctrines of God's Everlasting Love to His Elect*. See Gill, *Collection of Sermons and Tracts*, 3:198. For background on the exchange between Taylor and Gill, see Alan P. F. Sell, *Hinterland Theology: A Stimulus to Theological Construction* (Milton Keynes: Paternoster, 2008), 57–61.

[19] Gill, *Collection of Sermons and Tracts*, 3:198–203. Gill provided a similar argument against a more traditional understanding of justification by faith in his systematic theology. See Gill, *Complete Body*, 3:292–294.

[20] For Gill's indebtedness to the Reformed scholastic tradition, consider Muller, "John Gill and the Reformed Tradition," 51–68.

and wrought in them, but not offered. And as for the non-elect, grace is neither offered to them, nor bestowed on them, and therefore there can be no falsehood or hypocrisy, dissimulation or guile, nothing ludicrous or delusory in the divine conduct towards them, or anything which disproves God's act of preterition or reprobation.[21]

Gill provided two reasons for his rejection of Gospel offers in this statement. In regard to the elect, he feared that an offer of the Gospel might suggest that the elect must do something to obtain salvation. An offer might imply that a response is required. Rather than receiving an offer of the Gospel, the elect should instead realize that salvation is "bestowed upon them" in eternity.

In relation to the non-elect, Gill claimed that an offer of the Gospel does not comport with the doctrine of reprobation. Put simply, how might one offer the Gospel openly to all people when not all people are the recipients of saving grace? Gill therefore believed that universal offers of grace are insincere, both on the part of ministers who make the offers and, ultimately, on the part of God.

Rejecting Gospel offers, Gill preferred instead to speak of two distinct Gospel callings. An external call, which he described as the ministry of the word, goes out to all who have access to special revelation. It presents the Gospel message. On its own, however, it is incapable of granting salvation. For salvation to occur, one must receive an internal call, a drawing from the Holy Spirit. Such a calling goes to the elect only, often though not always, in conjunction with the ministry of the Word and it is always effectual.[22]

While this distinction between internal and external calling is not unique to Gill, it is interesting to note how his theology of eternal justification shaped his understanding of these two callings. The internal call goes only "to such who have a work of grace already begun in them."[23] With this statement, Gill referred to the fact that the elect, even before the internal calling of the Spirit, are the recipients of such spiritual blessings as eternal justification. The internal call therefore assists them in realizing their justified status by leading them to place their faith in Christ, thereby granting them passive justification. It also directs them to attend to the means of grace so that they might

---

[21] Gill, *Cause of God and Truth*, 289. Italics original. Gill offered several statements in his works that condemned the legitimacy of Gospel offers. Perhaps the most famous appeared in a polemical piece directed at John Wesley entitled *The Doctrine of Predestination Stated*. See Gill, *Collection of Sermons and Tracts*, 3:269–270.

[22] Gill mused that it would be possible for the elect to receive an effectual internal call to salvation without also receiving an external call. For his statements on this issue as well as his most thorough treatment of the internal and external calls, see Gill, *Complete Body*, 2:121–127.

[23] Gill, *Complete Body*, 2:122.

grow in sanctification.

Those who receive only the external call, by contrast, have no certain hope of salvation. They receive information about the Gospel as revealed in the ministry of the Word but, lacking any internal call of the Gospel, do not know whether they have been eternally justified. They gain no assurance from the external call.[24]

Most important, the internal call, given as it is to those who are already justified, carries with it an obligation to use "not only … the means of grace, but to partake of the blessings of grace." By contrast, the external call lacks such an obligation. Given to sinners in a "state of nature and unregeneracy," it is not

> a call to them to regenerate and convert themselves, of which there is no instance; and which is the pure work of the Spirit of God: nor to make their peace with God, which they cannot make by any thing they can do; and which is only made by the blood of Christ: nor to get an interest in Christ, which is not got, but given: nor to the exercise of evangelical grace, which they have not, and therefore can never exercise: nor to any spiritual vital acts, which they are incapable of, being natural men and dead in trespasses and sins.[25]

This distinction between callings is vital; it demonstrates Gill's denial of duty faith.

The external call only obliges its recipients to perform the "natural duties of religion." These duties include such activities as giving mental assent to the truths of the Gospel; the avoidance of sin, which Gill stated "even the light of nature dictates;" and prayers of gratitude. It also obliges its recipients to "the outward means of grace, and to make use of them." Describing these outward means of grace, Gill explained that they involved a duty "to read the holy scriptures, which have been the means of the conversion of some; to hear the word, and wait on the ministry of it, which may be blessed unto them, for the effectual calling of them." He further explained that, by attending to the means of grace, recipients of the external call receive an understanding of the Gospel and then "the whole" will be left "to the Spirit of God, to make application of it as

---

[24] This is the logical outflow of Gill's position, and he stated it explicitly in Gill, *Complete Body*, 2:121–131. See also the section in *The Cause of God and Truth*, in which Gill addressed conditional statements in preaching, that is, statements such as, "If you will repent, you will receive forgiveness." Concerning these statements and their relationship to the external call, Gill wrote, "I utterly deny that there is any promise of pardon made to the non-elect at all, not on any condition whatever." This fact means that no hope of assurance can emerge from the external call in and of itself. See Gill, *Cause of God and Truth*, 39.

[25] Gill, *Complete Body*, 2:122.

he shall think fit."[26]

In short, the external call directs its recipients to moral reform and religious activities so that they might potentially later receive an internal call. It does not explicitly issue a command to exercise faith in Christ; it only calls recipients to receive the ministry of the Word so that they "might wait on the ministry of it." As they wait, God may make application of the external call—that is, God may provide an internal call of the Gospel—as "he shall think fit."

One might wonder what value the external call has if it does not oblige its recipients to come to faith in Christ. Gill answered this question by pointing out some of the positive benefits it might convey. He stated that by it, many

> become more civilised, and more moral in their conversation, are reformed, as to their outward manners; and through a speculative knowledge of the gospel, escape the grosser pollutions of the world; and others are brought by it to a temporary faith, to believe for a while, to embrace the gospel notionally, to submit to the ordinances of it, make a profession of religion, by which means they become serviceable to support the interest of it.[27]

Therefore, though it "comports with the wisdom of God that there should be such an outward call of many who are not internally called," the external call can at least create a notional faith, and this faith can benefit individuals and even the broader society.[28]

Sensible sinners and repentance

While Gill's position on these matters seems sufficiently clear, two additional aspects of his thought merit brief attention because they further elucidate his convictions. When discussing the doctrine of repentance, he made a sharp division between legal repentance and evangelical repentance. Legal repentance involves only outward moral reform. According to Gill, the citizens of Nineveh during the ministry of Jonah illustrated this type of repentance. Although they temporarily modified their behavior, they experienced no lasting spiritual change, and they eventually suffered divine judgment. By contrast, evangelical repentance operates by divine grace. It is given only to the elect, and it assists

---

[26] Gill, *Complete Body*, 2:122–123.

[27] Gill, *Complete Body*, 2:124.

[28] Gill, *Complete Body*, 2:122–123.

them as they turn from sin as they receive passive justification.[29]

Gill made use of this distinction because it allowed him to account for Scripture passages that appear to call all people to repent and turn to God with saving faith. Given his denial of Gospel offers and duty faith, he could not recognize such universal calls to repentance, so he frequently claimed in his polemical writings and even in his biblical commentaries that broad calls to repentance were merely calls for individual or corporate moral reform, not calls pertaining to personal salvation.[30]

In order to preserve consistency with his convictions, then, he claimed that those who receive an external call have an obligation only to legal repentance, not to evangelical repentance.[31] They have no obligation to repent and trust Christ in a saving way; they must only modify their behavior and await an internal call. Only when they receive the internal call that assures them that they are among the elect are they responsible for evangelical repentance.

Gill also made a distinction between sensible sinners and non-elect sinners. He defined sensible sinners as elect people who have experienced regeneration but who have yet to receive full assurance. They are aware of their own sinfulness due to divine grace, and they are actively seeking a sense of passive justification in order to receive assurance. Sinners who are not among the elect, by contrast, are not the recipients of any spiritual blessings from God. They are therefore not fully aware of their need for justification because God has not revealed to them their sinful condition.

Gill stated that while he knew of "no exhortations to dead sinners [that is, the non-elect], to return and live" in Scripture, he acknowledged that pastors should "encourage and exhort sensible sinners to believe in Christ."[32] This statement merits attention because with it Gill maintained his conviction that offering the Gospel is inappropriate. He recommended here only that pastors exhort sensible sinners to trust in Christ. He did not instruct them to offer salvation to sensible sinners.

---

[29] For Gill's distinction between legal and evangelical repentance, see Gill, *Complete Body*, 2:368–371. See also *The Doctrines of God's Everlasting Love to the Elect* in Gill, *Collection of Sermons and Tracts*, 3:226–227. One should not confuse Gill's usage of these terms with that found in the work of John Calvin or James B. Torrance. Cf. John Calvin, *Institutes of the Christian Religion* 3.3.4, trans. Henry Beveridge (Edinburgh: The Calvin Translation Society, 1845), 2:154–155; Andrew Torrance, "John Calvin and James B. Torrance's Evangelical Vision of Repentance," *Participatio* 3 (2014): 126–147.

[30] See, for example, Gill, *Cause of God and Truth*, 64, 66, 287, 294; John Gill, *An Exposition of the Old Testament* (London: Mathews and Leigh, 1810), 6:91.

[31] Gill stated this explicitly in Gill, *Cause of God and Truth*, 307.

[32] Gill, *Cause of God and Truth*, 317. Gill's usage of the term "sensible sinners" carried with it different connotations than that of Puritan theologians such as John Bunyan. Cf. John Bunyan, *A Discourse Upon the Pharisee and Publican* (London: Blackie and Son, 1873), 187, 237.

Even more important, though, is the fact that with this statement Gill also revealed that he was not comfortable exhorting listeners to respond positively to the Gospel if he deemed them not elect. Careful readers will note that he claimed that he knew of no exhortations to trust the Gospel going out to uninterested or dead sinners and stated that one should provide Gospel exhortations only to sensible sinners.

Such a position often made Gill unwilling to recognize universal exhortations to trust in Christ or believe the Gospel, even when he found such exhortations in Scripture. Throughout his body of works and even in his sermons, he frequently interpreted universals calls to salvation as calls given only to sensible sinners and not calls given to all people.[33] This fact demonstrates just how chastened a view of evangelism he possessed.

Summary of Gill's soteriology

Gill desired to remove human participation from the act of salvation. He therefore constructed a theological system in which justification occurs as an immanent and eternal act of God. This system led him to reject the more traditional understanding of justification by faith. For Gill, faith only allows one to become aware of one's justified status; it is not a condition for the reception of actual justification. In his practical theology, he denied universal offers of the Gospel and even denied the legitimacy of duty faith. He formulated his convictions about sensible sinners, external and internal calls of the Gospel, and evangelical and legal repentance in light of this rejection of both Gospel offers and duty faith.

In Gill's understanding of evangelism, therefore, one makes a proclamation of the Gospel, an external call. Those who are already justified receive an internal call as they hear the Gospel proclaimed, and this internal call reveals to them that they need passive justification. Such people are sensible sinners. An evangelist can exhort these sensible sinners to trust in Christ to receive passive justification but cannot offer them salvation. In contrast, the non-elect receive only the external call to the Gospel and are obligated to perform only legal repentance—outward moral reform—and attend to the means of grace in the hopes that they might later receive an inward call to salvation. In Gill's system, one neither offers them the Gospel nor exhorts them to trust in the Gospel and must profess that they have no duty to believe the Gospel.

[33] See, for example, Gill, *Cause of God and Truth*, 38, 294, 317; Gill, *Complete Body*, 1:127, 531. It is revealing that Gill used the phrase "sensible sinners" 49 times in his New Testament commentaries and 80 times in his Old Testament commentaries. In many, though perhaps not all of these occurrences, he used the phrase to qualify what appear to be universal calls to respond to the Gospel. For example, when commenting on the apostolic preaching in Acts, he often stated that apostolic calls to receive salvation were given only to sensible sinners and not to all people. See, for example, John Gill, *An Exposition of the New Testament* (London: Mathews and Leigh, 1809), 2:168.

Assessing recent defenses of Gill—Thomas Nettles
Several noteworthy scholars attempt to defend Gill from the charge of hyper-Calvinism. The most significant are Thomas Nettles, Timothy George, and George Ella.[34] While their works display many commendable qualities, their contributions do suffer from a failure to appreciate just how Gill's soteriology shaped his understanding of Gospel preaching.

Nettles' research on Gill centers around two key publications. In *By His Grace and For His Glory*, a work that features his first significant published work on Gill, Nettles rightly acknowledges that Gill did not believe in the free offer of the Gospel.[35] However, he does claim that Gill "affirmed that it was the duty of all men to repent of sin and the duty of all who heard the Gospel to believe it."[36] He contends that this fact frees Gill from the charge of hyper-Calvinism.

In claiming that Gill did not deny duty faith, Nettles does not sufficiently explore Gill's soteriology. Though he surveys some aspects of Gill's thought—

---

[34] I select these historians and theologians because they have published significant pieces on Gill. Three noteworthy research projects that have not yet received publication do merit brief comment, however. Clive Jarvis provides a defense of Gill in his doctoral thesis on Particular Baptist life in Northamptonshire, and his analysis of Gill's contribution relies heavily on the work of George Ella. By critiquing Ella's convictions in this article, I can also interact with many of the claims made by Jarvis. See Clive Jarvis, "Growth in English Baptist Churches: With Special Reference to the Northamptonshire Particular Baptist Association (1770–1830)" (PhD diss., The University of Glasgow, 2001), 53–60; idem, "The Myth of Hyper-Calvinism?," in *Recycling the Past or Researching History?: Studies in Baptist Historiography and Myths*, ed. Philip E. Thompson and Anthony R. Cross, Studies in Baptist History and Thought, vol. 11 (Carlisle: Paternoster, 2005), 231–263.

Hong-Gyu Park offers hearty praise of Gill, but he focuses his research on such matters as Gill's doctrine of revelation. He does not consider Gill's soteriology or Gill's understanding of evangelism at length; it is therefore difficult to consider his research a full defense of Gill against the charge of hyper-Calvinism. See Park, "Grace and Nature," 30–74, 286–287. Park does fleetingly address Gill's doctrine of the *pactum salutis*. For my interaction with his work on this topic, see David Mark Rathel, "John Gill and the History of Redemption."

Jonathan White analyzes Gill's rather complex relationship with hyper-Calvinism in his doctoral dissertation. Regrettably, White employs an unnecessarily limited definition of hyper-Calvinism. He defines it as "the denial of the duty of unregenerate man to believe the gospel for salvation based on man's original lack of ability to believe the gospel for salvation." See Jonathan Anthony White, "A Theological and Historical Examination of John Gill's Soteriology in Relation to Eighteenth-Century Hyper-Calvinism" (PhD diss., The Southern Baptist Theological Seminary, 2010), 50. With this definition, White refers to the belief held by some early hyper-Calvinists that alleged that prelapsarian Adam possessed no ability to believe the Gospel. White's willingness to presuppose this definition when approaching Gill is unhelpful. Adamic inability was at best tangential to Gill's theological system; yet, Gill did passionately argue against Gospel offers and duty faith. Doctrines such as eternal justification—not an Adamic inability—motived Gill's understanding. White's thesis unfortunately does not take this fact into account. For more information on Gill and Adamic inability, see footnote 41 in this article.

[35] Thomas J. Nettles, *By His Grace and For His Glory: A Historical, Theological and Practical Study of the Doctrines of Grace in Baptist Life*, rev. ed. (Cape Coral, FL: Founders, 2006), 27–28, 47–48.

[36] Nettles, *By His Grace and For His Glory*, 42.

Gill's ordering of the divine decrees, his understanding of sanctification, and his pastoral ministry practices—he fails to probe Gill's desire to frame salvation as an eternal act of God that requires minimal human participation. Most notably, he does not address the doctrine of eternal justification in a significant manner even though it was a key component of Gill's theological project. This neglect causes Nettles to misrepresent Gill on the matter of duty faith. For example, Nettles cites a passage from Gill's *Cause of God and Truth* that he admits *prima facie* appears to deny duty faith. Gill wrote, "God does not require all men to believe in Christ; where he does it is according to the revelation he makes of them."[37] Nettles tries to soften the implications of this statement by arguing that Gill intended only "to highlight man's responsibility for that which is available to him."[38] Per Nettles, Gill wrote merely about those who have no access to the Gospel. He argued that such people are responsible only for what they receive through general revelation. Though Gill indeed addressed this particular topic in this passage, Nettles leaves unaddressed the next sentence in Gill's work. There Gill wrote, "Those who only have the outward ministry of the Word, unattended with the special illuminations of the Spirit of God, are obliged to believe no further than the external revelation they enjoy, reaches."[39] Put simply, Gill indeed stated that people only have a responsibility for the revelation that they receive; those who receive no access to the Gospel are accountable only for the general revelation that they have, but those who receive only the external call are obligated only to perform legal repentance and not trust in Christ for salvation. Gill makes this point even more explicit in the subsequent sentences in which he contrasts the mere legal obligations attending the external call with the salvific obligations attending the internal call. Nettles' argument, then, takes Gill out of context. It does so because Nettles has not sufficiently explored Gill's work on the external and internal callings as well as the soteriological convictions that undergird them.

In a subsequent publication, Nettles attempts to associate Gill with those who participated in the Evangelical Revival. A lack of adequate attention to Gill's soteriology also appears here, however, when Nettles implies several times that Gill held to the traditional understanding of justification by faith rather than the more eccentric position of eternal justification. This fact is trou-

---

[37] Nettles, *By His Grace and For His Glory*, 42. This quotation originally appears in Gill, *The Cause of God and Truth*, 307.

[38] Nettles, *By His Grace and For His Glory*, 42–43.

[39] Surprisingly, Nettles quotes this sentence but does not address it. See Nettles, *By His Grace and For His Glory*, 42–44.

bling given Gill's repeated protestations against justification by faith.[40] Most interesting is the fact that in this publication Nettles nuances his earlier defense of Gill. He admits, "There is a central point, however, in which he [Gill] appears to hold the [h]yper-Calvinist view [regarding duty faith]." He offers as evidence a quote from Gill's sermon entitled *Faith in God and His Word* in which Gill claimed, "Man never had in his power to have or to exercise [faith in Christ], no, not even in the state of innocence." Nettles then admits, "*Theoretically*, Gill held that the non-elect were not obligated to evangelical obedience, because the necessity of such obedience did not exist in unfallen humanity as deposited in Adam."[41] Surprisingly, despite this admission, Nettles remains cautious about labeling Gill a hyper-Calvinist, and he does not retract his earlier claim that Gill affirmed duty faith. He even continues to praise Gill, arguing that Gill's works exhibit "the central concerns and zeal of the Great Awakening."[42]

Nettles does so because he claims that Gill was only theoretically a hyper-Calvinist. He argues that in Gill's scheme "while many [people] exhibit … only a legal repentance and a historical faith, and the non-elect may not be theoretically obligated to the 'faith of God's elect,' ministers of the Gospel preach repentance and faith in a Gospel way."[43] Nettles reduces his argument to the contention that, even though Gill denied all people have an obligation to respond to the Gospel, at the practical level he still preached the Gospel, and this fact means that his hyper-Calvinism was merely hypothetical. I have the

---

[40] See Tom J. Nettles, "John Gill and the Evangelical Awakening" in Haykin, ed., *The Life and Thought of John Gill*, 136–137. Here Nettles praises Gill for defending the doctrine of justification by faith, but the form of justification Gill emphasized in *The Law Established by the Gospel*, the sermon that Nettles cites, was eternal justification. Indeed, *The Law Established* is one of the strongest sermons on eternal justification in the Gill corpus. See Gill, *Collection of Sermons and Tracts*, 1:200–216. In addition, when comparing Gill to John Wesley, Nettles associates Gill's understanding of justification with that of George Whitefield. See Nettles, "John Gill and the Evangelical Awakening," 137, n.163. While Whitefield, like Gill, would have rejected some of Wesley's convictions, Nettles makes no mention of the more unconventional aspects of Gill's theology of justification. Whitefield would have brokered no agreement with those. For instance, Gilbert Tennent, an occasional critic of Whitefield, once correctly noted Whitefield's rejection of eternal justification. See Thomas S. Kidd, *George Whitefield: America's Spiritual Founding Founder* (New Haven, CT: Yale University Press, 2014), 196–197.

[41] Nettles, "John Gill and the Evangelical Awakening," 153. Italics added. Some proponents of the no-offer position claimed that prelapsarian Adam had no ability to believe the Gospel. Gill's position on this matter is rather complex, but there is no doubt that he did at times affirm Adamic inability. See Gill, *Cause of God and Truth*, 307. Nevertheless, Gill's belief in an Adamic inability did not profoundly shape his convictions about Gospel offers and duty faith—his views on salvation in eternity did. Andrew Fuller offered helpful analysis of Gill's rather contradictory statements concerning Adamic inability in *The Complete Works of the Rev. Andrew Fuller*, ed. Joseph Belcher (1845, Harrisonburg, VA: Sprinkle Publications, 1988), 2:421.

[42] Nettles, "John Gill and the Evangelical Awakening," 170.

[43] Nettles, "John Gill and the Evangelical Awakening," 154.

utmost respect for Nettles and his contribution to Baptist scholarship, but I find this argument is unpersuasive. As noted, Gill's commentaries and sermons reveal that his soteriological convictions often caused him to interpret Scripture in such a way that he minimized universal calls to respond to the Gospel. Such an act displays that he held his principles at more than just a theoretical level; they regularly affected his preaching and exposition of Scripture.

The differences between Gill's ministry and that of the evangelists of the Evangelical Revival, those to whom Nettles wishes to compare Gill, are therefore stark. Gill constructed a ministry philosophy that emphasized encouraging only sensible sinners to respond to the Gospel and often eschewed giving Gospel exhortations to all people. The evangelists of the Evangelical Revival did not.

With Nettles, then, readers find a contradictory portrayal of Gill. While throughout his works Nettles maintains that Gill denied Gospel offers, in one work he claims that Gill did not deny that all people have an obligation to respond to the Gospel. In another, without retracting this claim, he admits that Gill likely held to the hyper-Calvinist tenet of denying duty faith. He deems this point irrelevant, though, and incorrectly believes that it did not shape Gill's ministry. Nettles could have avoided these errors by more completely examining how deeply Gill's soteriology formed his thought and practice.

Assessing recent defenses of Gill—Timothy George
Out of all of Gill's defenders, the respected Baptist theologian Timothy George offers the most interesting arguments, yet he is also the most restrained in his praise of Gill. While he does not label Gill a hyper-Calvinist, he holds this conclusion rather tentatively, and in several places admits that Gill's theology possessed unhelpful tendencies.[44] He especially criticizes the dangers posed by Gill's doctrine of eternal justification. He writes that with eternal justification Gill stressed the "priority of justification over faith," that "the doctrine was a stumbling block to many who could not square it with the necessity of conversion as a personal experience of grace," and that it was a "perilous teaching, insofar as it encouraged sinners to think of themselves as actually justified regardless of their personal response to Christ and the Gospel." The *Second London Confession*, a document that drew heavily from the *Westminster Confession of Faith*, explicitly rejected eternal justification, and George remarks, "Happily, on this controversial issue most Particular Baptists followed the fathers of the

---

[44] George writes that the historic presentation of Gill as a hyper-Calvinist is "a hasty judgment that *may* need to be reconsidered." Italics added. He further explains that, though he does not count Gill as a hyper-Calvinist in the vein of Hussey or Brine, "We cannot quite exonerate Gill of all responsibility in the fostering of an atmosphere in which the forthright promulgation of the missionary mandate of the church was seen to be a threat to, rather than an extension of, the gospel of grace." (George, "John Gill," 28–29).

Second London Confession rather than John Gill."[45]

George's willingness to address Gill's statements on eternal justification is commendable. Unfortunately, he fails to explore how Gill's stance on eternal justification shaped his understanding of duty faith and evangelism. George does not address the concept of duty faith in Gill's thought, a disappointing omission in an otherwise excellent essay. He also neglects Gill's statements on such matters as evangelical repentance and sensible sinners, convictions that originated primarily from Gill's doctrine of eternal justification.

One receives the impression in George's work that Gill proclaimed the Gospel clearly with no constraint; however, by not connecting Gill's doctrine of enteral justification to its implications for evangelism, such a portrayal is not entirely accurate. In one place, George quotes from an ordination sermon that he claims demonstrates Gill's healthy evangelistic ministry. During the sermon, Gill charged the ministry candidate:

> Souls sensible to sin and danger, and who are crying out, What shall we do to be saved? you are to observe, and point out Christ the tree of life to them; and say ... Believe on the Lord Jesus Christ and thou shalt be saved, Acts 16:31. Your work is to lead men, under a sense of sin and guilt, to the blood of Christ, shed for many for the remission of sin, and in this name you are to preach the forgiveness to them.[46]

Such a quote does not demonstrate George's point. One should note to whom Gill instructs the young ministry candidate to direct his evangelistic appeals—to "souls *sensible* to sin and danger." One therefore finds Gill's doctrine of sensible sinners on full display. George goes on to refer to additional passages in which Gill warned young ministers that if they did not preach Christ, the blood of their listeners would be on their hands. He further quotes a text from Gill's *The Cause of God and Truth* in which Gill stated that ministers are to "preach the gospel of salvation to all men, and declare, that whosoever believes shall be saved: for this they are commissioned to do."[47] While one can express gratitude for Gill's willingness to call ministers to preach the Gospel, when assessing such quotations one must remember Robert Oliver's helpful remarks on Gill's preaching. Oliver explains that a

---

[45] George, "John Gill," 26–27.

[46] George, "John Gill," 28. This quote appears in Gill's *The Doctrine of the Cherubim Opened and Explained*. See Gill, *Sermons and Tracts*, 2:36–37. George perhaps misses the full context of Gill's statement because he draws the quote from a secondary source, Olin C. Robison, "The Legacy of John Gill," *Baptist Quarterly* 24, no. 3 (1971): 111–125.

[47] George, "John Gill," 28. The original quote appears in Gill, *The Cause of God and Truth*, 303.

> cause of confusion arises from the popular view that hyper-Calvinists are never concerned for the salvation of sinners ... Gill was one [who possessed such a concern] and examples can be produced of him expressing a concern for such and pressing those who *were awakened* to turn and seek salvation. His hyper-Calvinism appears in the absence of direct exhortations and appeals to the unconverted to turn from their sin in repentance and cast themselves upon Christ.[48]

Oliver rightly explains that the preaching of the Gospel is not the issue in the debate over Gill's hyper-Calvinism; hyper-Calvinists such as Joseph Hussey and John Brine both preached the Gospel. Instead, the issue is how one understands Gospel offers and duty faith as well as the accompanying doctrines of sensible sinners and evangelical repentance. Considering this fact, merely pointing out Gill's charge to preach the Gospel is not sufficient.

In fact, one must interpret Gill's call to "preach the gospel of salvation to all men, and declare, that whosoever believes shall be saved" within its proper context. That statement appears in a work that contains some of the strongest statements against the legitimacy of Gospel offers and duty faith in Gill's corpus. In the very sentence from which George draws this quote, Gill denied Gospel offers by writing that the Gospel minister "ought not to offer and tender salvation to any." Even more troubling, in the sentences immediately preceding it, Gill denied duty faith when he wrote, "None are bound to believe in Christ, but such to whom a revelation of him is made and according to the revelation is the faith they are obliged to." He explained that people who "have only an external revelation of him by the ministry of the word"—that is, people who hear the Gospel preached through the external call but do not receive an internal call of the Spirit—are required to believe "no more than is included in that revelation, as that Jesus is the Son of God, the Messiah, who died and rose again, and is the Saviour of sinners etc., but not that he died for them, or that he is their Saviour."[49] The external call can only obligate its recipients to give mental assent to the truth of the Gospel; apart from the internal call the preaching of the Gospel cannot appeal for any person to exercise faith.

One can likely account for George's misreading of Gill by noting that, for his statements on Gill's convictions on evangelism, he relies heavily on the work

---

[48] Robert Oliver, "John Gill," in *The British Particular Baptists, 1638–1910*, ed. Michael A.G. Haykin (Springfield, MO: Particular Baptist Press, 1998), 1:161–162. I have added italics to this quote to highlight the people for whom Gill expressed concern—those who "were awakened," that is, those who were sensible sinners. See my remarks on Gill's doctrine of sensible sinners in this article for more information.

[49] Gill, *The Cause of God and Truth*, 303.

of Thomas Nettles.[50] As demonstrated, Nettles does not address Gill's doctrine of eternal justification in a significant manner, and this fact leads him to misinterpret Gill's convictions about evangelism. Though George explores Gill's doctrine of eternal justification and rightly sees its dangers, when he assesses Gill's evangelistic practices he relies on a source that does not do so, and the incorporation of Nettles' material gives George's presentation of Gill an unbalanced feel. George is right on Gill's understanding of eternal justification, but he is wrong in assuming that eternal justification had no relevance for Gill's understating of Gospel proclamation.

George's strong reliance on Nettles becomes especially evident in the several instances in which he uses Nettles to assert that Gill held to different convictions than Joseph Hussey, a man whom George considers a genuine hyper-Calvinist.[51] Nettles' chief argument for distancing Gill from Hussey is his contention that Gill did not consistently argue that prelapsarian Adam possessed an inability to believe the Gospel. Nettles identifies this understanding of Adamic inability as one of hyper-Calvinism's key features. He appears to assume that if Gill did not hold to an important hyper-Calvinist tenet associated with Hussey then Gill might remain free from the charge of hyper-Calvinism.

This comparison with Hussey has little relevance, however, because Hussey never explicitly argued for Adam's incapacity to believe the Gospel. That teaching arrived later in the hyper-Calvinist controversy, primarily around the time of the Modern Question debate. Hussey's hyper-Calvinism originated instead from a commitment to eternal justification—interestingly, the same theological position that powered Gill's hyper-Calvinism.

Assessing recent defenses of Gill—George Ella
George Ella is perhaps the most passionate of Gill's defenders. Interestingly, though Ella expresses great displeasure with those who label Gill a hyper-Calvinist, in his most recent work he does not deny the fact that Gill rejected Gospel offers and duty faith. Ella therefore helps to confirm—and does not disprove—that Gill held to such convictions. In addition, Ella holds convictions similar to those of Gill, and he presents Gill as a model for contemporary pas-

---

[50] While George cites Nettles several times, he cites him twice in reference to Gill's relationship with hyper-Calvinism. Both citations carry great weight in his argument. See George, "John Gill," 28, n.64; 29, n.68; 364–365.

[51] George, "John Gill," 29, n.68.

tors to emulate, hoping that they too will reject Gospel offers and duty faith.[52] The question raised by Ella's work, then, becomes that of normativity—is the no-offer, no-duty faith position normative, or does it represent a departure from traditional Reformed soteriology and deserve a descriptor such as hyper-Calvinism? The latter is correct, and throughout his works Ella does not convincingly demonstrate the contrary.

A concluding word
John Gill offered a soteriology that magnified the role of divine grace and minimized the significance of human action. His doctrine of eternal justification illustrates this fact well. Gill's soteriology led him to deny the legitimacy of Gospel offers and duty faith, and recent attempts to argue otherwise remain unpersuasive. Gill's final position, then, accords well with the theology that many of his critics label hyper-Calvinism.

---

[52] George M. Ella, *The Free Offer and The Call of the Gospel* (Durham: Go Publications, 2001), 51–53, 62, 66–67. Ella in one place calls those who espouse the Gospel-offer position—that is, the typical evangelical stance toward Gospel preaching—as "highly liberal." See his *The Free Offer and The Call of the Gospel*, 23, 66. Compare Ella's manner of defending Gill in this more recent work with the approach he took in his earlier pieces. See, for example, Ella, "John Gill and the Charge of Hyper-Calvinism," 160–170; idem, *John Gill and the Cause of God and Truth* (Durham: Go Publications, 1995); idem, *John Gill and Justification from Eternity: A Tercentenary Appreciation (1697–1997)* (Durham: Go Publications, 1998).

"Be reconciled to trying disciplines": Andrew Fuller's pastorate at Soham, 1775–1782

Peter J. Morden

Peter Morden is the Senior Pastor/Team Leader, Cornerstone Baptist Church, Leeds, England, and a Distinguished Visiting Scholar at Spurgeon's College, London.

Introduction

John Webster Morris once commented that the famous Baptist minister, theologian and missionary statesman Andrew Fuller "arose out of obscurity."[1] The details of Fuller's early life certainly support this judgement. He was born on February 6, 1754, at Wicken, a tiny village in Fenland, Cambridgeshire, in a ramshackle farmhouse which was finally demolished in 1861.[2] He was the youngest son of Robert Fuller and Philippa Gunton. Robert was a tenant farmer, eking out a living by renting and working a succession of small and, it appears, not especially profitable farmsteads. In 1761 the family moved to the slightly larger settlement of Soham, just two and a half miles from Wicken.

Both parents were Dissenters, although Robert was markedly less committed than his wife. Philippa became a member of the Particular (Calvinistic)

---

[1] John W. Morris, *Memoirs of the Life and Death of the Rev. Andrew Fuller*, 2nd ed. (London: Wightman and Cramp, 1826), 17.

[2] It was painted by Andrew Fuller's son, Andrew Gunton Fuller, in the year it was pulled down. The original painting is held at Fuller Baptist Church, Kettering.

Baptist church at Soham, and the whole family attended.[3] Her own mother, also called Philippa, had actually been one of the six founding members of the fellowship.[4] The church had remained small throughout its life. It was isolated geographically from other fellowships that would have been supportive, an isolation compounded by the Particular Baptist stress on the independency of each local congregation. By 1775 and the commencement of Fuller's pastorate, the church was in a parlous state, trying to recover from a lacerating dispute which had almost forced its closure.[5] Fuller was only 21 years of age and had little by way of formal education.[6] His pastorate at Soham was to last seven years. His time there was never easy and an already difficult situation deteriorated markedly after a change in his theology led to a corresponding change in his preaching. He faced much painful opposition from within the church. To obscurity, then, can be added hardship and struggle. The young pastor's beginnings in ministry were difficult indeed.

This paper draws on various sources, including previously untapped autograph manuscript material and some newly-deciphered shorthand notes of Fuller's farewell sermons, to chart the course of his pastorate at Soham. The focus is on his practical ministry rather than the theology which underpinned it. True, the period in question was crucial for his theological development. However, the tectonic shifts in his thinking have been delineated in some detail elsewhere,[7] and I have written about them at length myself in a number of places.[8] Less well mapped are the corresponding changes to his practical ministry that occurred during this period. So, although theology does feature in the following account (it would be almost impossible to write about Fuller's Soham pastorate without reference to theology), the reasons for the sea-change in his thinking are not given an extended treatment here. Rather, it is the outworking

---

[3] John Ryland, Jr., *The Work of Faith, the Labour of Love, and the Patience of Hope Illustrated in the Life and Death of the Rev. Andrew Fuller*, 2nd ed. (London: Button and Son, 1818), 8–10.

[4] Soham Baptist Church Book, 1752–1868 (Cambridgeshire County Archive [N/B–Soham]), 1.

[5] For this dispute, see Peter J. Morden, *The Life and Ministry of Andrew Fuller (1754-1815)* (Milton Keynes: Paternoster, 2015), 34–35. The main years of controversy were 1770–1772, but the effects of the dispute were still being felt in 1775.

[6] For Fuller's early life, including his conversion and experiences at Soham Baptist Church prior to his becoming pastor, see Morden, *Fuller*, 11–37.

[7] See, e.g., Michael A.G. Haykin, *One Heart and One Soul: John Sutcliff of Olney, his friends and his times* (Durham: Evangelical Press, 1994), 133–152; Chris Chun, *The Legacy of Jonathan Edwards in the Theology of Andrew Fuller* (Leiden: Brill, 2012), 32–65.

[8] As well as Morden, *Fuller*, 47–67, see Morden, "Andrew Fuller and the *Gospel Worthy of All Acceptation*," in *Pulpit and People: Studies in Eighteenth-Century Baptist Life and Thought*, ed. John H.Y. Briggs (Milton Keynes: Paternoster, 2009), 128–151.

of those changes that are subject to special scrutiny. It will be argued that what happened in this obscure and difficult context laid the foundations for Fuller's later ministry, a ministry which was to have global significance.

Soham Baptist and the Northamptonshire Association
Fuller's Soham pastorate at least began in positive fashion. Barely one month after his induction, the church made a decision that would greatly lessen its isolation. On June 8, 1775, Soham applied to join the Northamptonshire Association of Particular Baptist churches, an application that was made by the "unanimous consent" of the membership.[9] This move was most likely prompted by a recommendation from Robert Hall, Sr., pastor of Arnesby Baptist Church, Leicestershire.[10] Hall had given the "charge" at the new pastor's induction service and was an important figure in Association life. Soham was, of course, in Cambridgeshire, but the Northamptonshire Association included churches, like Hall's own, from outside the county.

In applying to join this Association, Soham was not giving up its status as an independent church. In common with other English Particular Baptist churches they strongly affirmed the "independency" which was the bedrock of their ecclesiology; indeed, there is a comment to this effect in Fuller's handwritten "Narration of the Dealings of God … with the Baptist Church of Christ at Soham," made alongside his record of their application.[11] Yet, whilst guarding their autonomy as a congregation, Fuller wanted Soham to be in active fellowship with other churches. The application to join the Northamptonshire Association was duly successful. It is unlikely that either pastor or people comprehended the impact joining this wider body would have on their church. The Association was relatively new, having been formed only in 1764. It was, as John Briggs states, the "archetype of the new associations, born out of the Evangelical Revival."[12] The Soham church had previously been impervious to the influence of the Revival, which had reshaped the religious scene in Britain from the 1730s and was characterised by, amongst other things, applied

---

[9] "A Narration of the Dealings of God in a way of Providence with the Baptist Church of Christ at Soham, from the Year 1770" (Autograph ms., Cambridgeshire County Archives [N/B–Soham R70/20]), 25.

[10] For Hall, see John Ryland, Jr, *Memoirs of Robert Hall of Arnsby [sic]. With a Brief History of the Baptist Church*, 2nd ed.; rev. ed. J.A. Jones (London: James Paul, 1850).

[11] "Narration," 24. Fuller was stating that the pastors involved in his ordination and induction "Disclaim'd all authority and superintendency over or among us." We maintain "that form of church government called Independency," he declared. The word "independency" is written in especially large letters, presumably for emphasis.

[12] John H.Y. Briggs, *English Baptists of the Nineteenth Century* (Didcot, Oxfordshire: Baptist Historical Society, 1994), 203.

evangelistic preaching. This was about to change. For Soham Baptist Church and for Fuller himself, a new era had begun.[13]

The Association only met officially once a year, in either May or June. Given the wide geographical spread of member churches and the atrocious state of many of the eighteenth-century roads, gathering more frequently would have been extremely difficult. Yet, through these annual meetings Fuller came into contact with a number of evangelical Baptist ministers. Spiritual friendships developed, nurtured by smaller, informal get-togethers and regular correspondence. Hall, Sr. was twenty-six years older than Fuller and acted as a sort of spiritual mentor to the younger man. The Soham pastor also got to know others of a similar age to him. The most significant of these were John Ryland, Jr., who was then at Northampton, and John Sutcliff, who had recently settled at the Baptist church at Olney, Buckinghamshire. Ryland had been influenced in his own ministry by his friendship with the evangelical Anglican clergyman John Newton, and Sutcliff had been shaped by his training at Bristol Baptist Academy, which was a seedbed for evangelical thinking. Ryland, Sutcliff and Fuller became lifelong friends. These rich spiritual friendships would contribute to a radical recasting of Fuller's approach to ministry.[14]

Soham Baptist Church to November 1779

In common with all Association churches, Soham had to write a report which would be read out at the yearly formal meeting. These "annual letters" gave an overview of congregational life for the previous twelve months as well as up-to-date membership statistics. The letters from Soham survive and are extremely helpful in gauging the state of the fellowship during Fuller's ministry, although it should be remembered they were written for public consumption. It appears the pastor composed them himself and, as the church's principal "messenger" at the "annual Association," he would have read them out to the gathering.[15] His

---

[13] For the resistance of many Particular Baptist churches to Revival influences, with a special focus on Soham, see Morden, *Fuller*, 25–28.

[14] For Sutcliff, see Michael A.G. Haykin, "A Habitation of God, through the Spirit: John Sutcliff (1752–1814) and the Revitalization of the Calvinistic Baptists in the Late-Eighteenth Century," *Baptist Quarterly* 34, no.7 (July 1992): 304–319. For Ryland, see Christopher Crocker, "The Life and Legacy of John Ryland Jr. (1753–1825)—a Man of Considerable Usefulness—an Historical Biography" (PhD thesis, University of Aberdeen/Bristol Baptist College, 2018). Ryland, Jr.'s father, John Ryland, Sr., was also a Baptist minister, as was Robert Hall's son, Robert Hall, Jr. In this paper, "Ryland" and "Hall" are always Ryland, Jr. and Hall, Sr. respectively.

[15] "Annual Letters on the State of the Ch[urch] sent to the Association from the year 1776," (Cambridgeshire County Archives, Autograph mss. [N/B–Soham R70/20]). There are eight letters in all, covering the years 1776–83, inserted at the back of the "Narration." The last letter was not composed by Fuller although it does refer to his time at the church. The others are in his handwriting.

first such meeting was at Olney on May 28, 1776, and it was probably there that he first met Sutcliff and Ryland.[16] Soham's 1776 letter stated that as a church they were "not without complaints" because of their "unfruitfulness in religion and proneness to evil." Nevertheless, "sinners [had been] awakened and some of them, we trust, bro"t to the knowledge of [Christ]." The church was both "increased" and "built up." In the course of the year, two members had died but six had joined, with the total membership now standing at thirty-five.[17] The church was small but under Fuller's ministry it was experiencing some growth. Unfortunately, the following year the news was less positive. The Association was informed that in the previous twelve months at Soham one member had been excluded and "none added."[18] They were able to report two better years numerically in 1778 and 1779, with more additions than deaths and with no one excluded or leaving for other reasons. By May 1779 the number of members had risen to forty-five.[19] However, this was as large as the membership would get during Fuller's pastorate.

Behind these headline figures, ministry at Soham was tough. The 1779 letter made mention of "unhappy differences between individuals."[20] The more detailed and less guarded "Narration" reveals that a range of behavioural issues were regularly brought before the monthly church members' meeting. For example, in 1776 a member was admonished for "repeatedly … speaking falsehoods" and suspended from communion for a number of months.[21] In 1777 the same member was reprimanded for being repeatedly drunk and was excluded. Drunkenness appears to have been a particular problem for the church, for 1777 also saw a different member "publickly examin'd" in respect of his heavy drinking. This second man confessed, expressed sorrow and explained he had been "strangely overtaken."[22] Such issues were not uncommon in eighteenth-century Particular Baptist life and they were invariably dealt with by

---

[16] So Morris, *Fuller*, 33–34. At the close of his life, Fuller reminisced that he became "acquainted" with Sutcliff first, then with Ryland "soon after." It may be that he got to know Sutcliff fairly well at the 1776 Association, but only spoke briefly to Ryland on that occasion. See Andrew Fuller, Letter to My Dear Friend, February, 1815, in "Typescript Andrew Fuller Letters," transcribed by Joyce A. Booth, superintended by Ernest A. Payne (Angus Library, Regent's Park College, Oxford, 4/5/1 and 4/5/2), (4/5/2).

[17] Letter 1, May 1776 (Association at Olney, Bucks).

[18] Letter 2, May 1777 (Association at Okeham [Oakham], Rutland).

[19] Letter 3, May 1778 (Association at Leicester), six added, one died; Letter 4, May 1779 (Association at Northampton), seven added, one died.

[20] Letter 4, May 1779.

[21] "Narration," 26.

[22] "Narration," 27.

the church meeting. Church minute books show that members were regularly censured for the same sorts of reasons, with Robert Robinson's growing and lively Particular Baptist church in nearby Cambridge just one example.[23] So, neither the problems at Soham or the way they were handled were unusual.[24] Nevertheless, the behaviour of some in the fellowship was dispiriting for Fuller, for his robust physical appearance belied a man of deep and "sensitive feelings" who could be easily hurt.[25]

In December 1776 Andrew Fuller had married Sarah Gardiner, a member at Soham. Morris described her as "an amiable woman … greatly beloved by her connections."[26] Andrew and Sarah's relationship seems to have been strong, although it was marked by tragedy. They had four children in the first four years of their marriage but three of them died very young.[27] Both parents were struck with grief at the loss of these children.[28] They also had serious financial concerns. Fuller's stipend was a paltry £13 a year. He did receive an additional £5 from the Particular Baptist Fund in London and an extra £3 for preaching some sermons in a neighbouring village. Yet his yearly income was still inadequate to live on. Attempts to supplement this, first by running a small shop and then a school, failed. The Fullers found it very difficult to manage and their situation looked as if it would be untenable long term.[29]

Soham and high Calvinism

The dominant theology at Soham was that of "high Calvinism" or, as Fuller would later call it, "false Calvinism."[30] Put simply, high Calvinists exalted the

---

[23] *Church Book: St Andrew's Street Baptist Church, Cambridge 1720–1832*, ed. Leonard G. Champion, L.E. Addicott and K.A.C. Parsons (Didcot: Baptist Historical Society, 1991). See, e.g., the entry for February 18, 1773 (page 50).

[24] Cf. Alan P.F. Sell et al., *Protestant Nonconformist Texts: Volume 2: The Eighteenth Century* (Aldershot: Ashgate, 2006), 389, and the editorial comment that many eighteenth-century church books, both Independent and Baptist, "devote a significant proportion of their space to disciplining matters."

[25] Andrew Gunton Fuller, *Men Worth Remembering: Andrew Fuller* (London: Hodder and Stoughton, 1882), 44.

[26] Morris, *Fuller*, 34.

[27] Ryland, *Fuller*, 44, 88. Cf. Morris, *Fuller*, 34.

[28] Three children had died before January 1781. See Ryland, *Fuller*, 88. Later, Sarah would experience considerable struggles with her mental health.

[29] Andrew Gunton Fuller, "Memoir" in *The Complete Works of the Rev. Andrew Fuller*, ed. Andrew Gunton Fuller, rev. ed. Joseph Belcher, 3rd ed. (1845, Harrisonburg VA: Sprinkle Publications, 1988), I:1, 18–19; Ryland, *Fuller*, 44. Morris, *Fuller*, 34, states Fuller stopped running the school in April 1780.

[30] Ryland, *Fuller*, 11.

sovereignty of God in salvation in ways that greatly minimised the importance of human response.[31] In particular, it was no one's "duty" to repent and believe the gospel, since total depravity rendered such a response impossible. Building on these shaky theological foundations, high Calvinists refused to "offer" the gospel freely to all. As Fuller himself later put it, preachers said nothing to "sinners … inviting them to apply to Christ for salvation."[32] Such invitations to trust in Christ were, high Calvinists claimed, a nonsense since faith was not a "duty" and the "elect" would come to believe anyway in God's good time. Furthermore, applied evangelistic preaching was dangerous because it encouraged false professions of faith that could sully the purity of the church. In summary, it was considered both theologically wrong and practically dangerous to "offer" the gospel openly and freely to all. Invitational gospel preaching was rejected.

The previous pastor at Soham, John Eve, had been a convinced high Calvinist who, according to Fuller, had "little or nothing to say to the unconverted."[33] This was the theology the young pastor had inherited, and consequently he did not invite people to put their trust in Christ in his preaching. However, from the beginning of his ministry he was uncertain about this approach, and his doubts steadily grew. Between the years 1775 and 1779 he went on a journey that led to his decisive rejection of high Calvinism as a theological system. As already noted, this article does not especially focus on what influenced this seismic shift in his thinking, but it is important to at least note some of the central factors. The influence of Fuller's friends, especially the aforementioned Hall, Ryland and Sutcliff, were crucial. All three had rejected high Calvinism in favour of an evangelical approach. For them, faith *must* be a duty. If God had commanded all to have faith then it was surely the duty of all to believe, and—crucially—the corresponding duty of preachers to urge them to do so. These men had each been influenced in their approach by the New England philosopher-theologian Jonathan Edwards, a central figure in transatlantic eighteenth-century Evangelicalism. Fuller read Edwards for himself, especially his seminal *Freedom of the Will*, which had been recommended to him by Hall. Edwardsean thinking was clearly vital for Fuller.[34] There was continuity

---

[31] Keith S. Grant, *Andrew Fuller and the Evangelical Renewal of Pastoral Theology* (Milton Keynes: Paternoster, 2013), 28. Grant's brief survey of high Calvinism (26–28) is extremely well done. High Calvinism was a departure from earlier Puritan emphases that sought to hold divine sovereignty and human responsibility in more careful balance. For the genesis of high Calvinism, see Morden, *Fuller*, 16–17.

[32] Ryland, *Fuller*, 31–32.

[33] Ryland, *Fuller*, 11.

[34] For the text, see Jonathan Edwards, *Freedom of the Will*, The Works of Jonathan Edwards, vol. 1, ed. Paul Ramsey (New Haven, CT: Yale University Press, 1985), 135–440. For the influence of Edwards on Fuller, see Morden, *Fuller*, 60–65.

with the sixteenth and seventeenth centuries as well, for he also engaged with Reformed and Puritan authors as he considered what his approach to ministry should be.[35] Nevertheless, he was especially being shaped by forces associated with the Evangelical Revival.

A further reason for Fuller's change of theological tack is one I particularly want to highlight: his biblicism. Commitment to the authority of the Bible was one of the hallmarks of eighteenth-century Evangelicalism, although it had of course been present in sixteenth- and seventeenth-century Protestantism as well.[36] Fuller's own biblicism can be seen by the way he engaged with other literature he was reading. For example, in 1775, he read a pamphlet that he later said was crucial in the development of his thought.[37] The tract was written by an Independent, that is, Congregationalist, minister, Abraham Taylor, although when it first appeared in 1742 it was published anonymously.[38] Taylor's tract asked whether the unconverted have a duty to believe the gospel, answering in the affirmative. The pamphlet was obviously relevant to Fuller's concerns but, by his own account, as he worked his way through the opening pages he was "but little impressed with [Taylor's] reasonings."[39] Moreover, the Congregationalist's abrasive style (he had been accused of promoting "bigotry"),[40] did not endear him to Fuller. His response changed, however, when he came to a passage in which the Independent cited a string of biblical texts, specifically some of those which show John the Baptist, the apostles and Christ himself directly addressing the unconverted. Taylor was able to show, in a way that Fuller was unable to answer, that New Testament figures repeatedly challenged the "ungodly" to spiritual repentance and faith.[41] The impact on Fuller was great. In the following months he read and re-read the relevant Scripture passages. "The

---

[35] For example, he read widely in the works of John Owen. See Morden, *Fuller*, 53–56, especially, 54–55. Fuller's thinking is set out in "Thoughts of the Power of Man to do the Will of God" (Autograph ms., Southern Baptist Theological Seminary, Louisville, KY [Q98.F95]). There is a handwritten note on the first page of the manuscript, probably by Fuller's son Andrew Gunton Fuller, stating the paper was written in 1777 or 1778.

[36] David W. Bebbington, *Evangelicalism in Modern Britain: A History from the 1730s to the 1980s* (London: Unwin Hyman, 1989), 12–14.

[37] Ryland, *Fuller*, 34, 37.

[38] See Geoffrey F. Nuttall, "Northamptonshire and the Modern Question," in Geoffrey F. Nuttall, *Studies in English Dissent* (Weston Rhyn, Shropshire: Quinta, 2002), 207–208.

[39] Ryland, *Fuller*, 37. Cf. Gunton Fuller, *Fuller*, 42.

[40] By the influential Independent minister Philip Doddridge. See Nuttall, "Northamptonshire and the Modern Question," 221.

[41] Ryland, *Fuller*, 37. Cf. Gunton Fuller, *Fuller*, 42.

more I read and thought," he said, "the more I doubted the justice of my former views."[42] He could not forget these texts, nor help feeling that they exposed his preaching as "anti-scriptural and defective in many respects."[43] The point is not so much that Taylor influenced Fuller, rather that the passages Taylor cited did. Thus, Fuller's commitment to biblical authority was vitally important to his change of views.

Soham Baptist from December 1779 to September 1781
By the late 1770s Fuller had become convinced his pulpit ministry needed to change. He introduced direct appeals to the unconverted into his preaching late in 1779. The result was, unsurprisingly, consternation and "bitterness of spirit" at Soham.[44] It is important to note that not all the members turned against him. Ryland wrote that, "A tinge of false Calvinism infected some of the people, who were inclined to find fault with his ministry, as it became more searching and practical, and as he freely enforced the indefinite calls of the gospel."[45] Fuller himself wrote of "reproach," but added that this was only true of "some" rather than all.[46] Probably we should think of opposition from a significant minority of the members. Nevertheless, this opposition was determined, vociferous and—in such a small church—highly disruptive. Furthermore, the pastor found the personal nature of some the attacks on him very hard to deal with.[47] Ryland, working with free access to all Fuller's private papers, was able to date the beginning of the opposition precisely, to December 1779.[48]

We should not imagine an "overnight" *volte-face* in Fuller's pulpit ministry, with high Calvinism shaping his methodology one week and full-fledged appeals to the unconverted being given the next. Instead, his new mode of preaching developed over a number of months. In July of 1780 he was still worried that his sermons were not searching and practical enough. He confided in his diary, "I find, by conversation today, with one seemingly in dying circumstances, that but little of my preaching has been suited to her case." Fuller's conclusion was that an increased amount of time spent visiting the people

---

[42] Ryland, *Fuller*, 37.

[43] Ryland, *Fuller*, 34.

[44] Gunton Fuller, *Fuller*, 45.

[45] Ryland, *Fuller*, 44; cf. Morris, *Fuller*, 34.

[46] In the "Narration," 47, Fuller referred to the "reproach of some and the indifference of others."

[47] "Narration," 46.

[48] Ryland, *Fuller*, 44.

of the village would make his messages more "experimental" and applied.[49] Yet still he struggled to break decisively from his past as far as his practical ministry was concerned.

Fuller's behaviour towards his father provides further evidence of this continuing struggle. By the close of January, 1781, Robert Fuller was dying. He had never come into membership at Soham, remaining only a "hearer" or regular attender. The son believed Robert was not a Christian and agonised over his father's "eternal state." Despite his new approach to ministry he was hesitant to speak evangelistically to Robert, although his heart was "much drawn out" in prayer to God for him.[50] By January 26, with his father's health clearly failing, the son plucked up some courage with the following conversation recorded in Fuller's diary:

> *Son.* "Have you any outgoings of soul, father, to the Lord?" *Father.* "Yes, my dear, I have." *Son.* "Well, father, the Lord is rich in mercy to all that call upon him. This is great encouragement." *Father.* "Yes, my child, so it is; and I know, if I be saved, it must be by him alone. I have nothing to recommend me to his favour ... but my hopes are very small."[51]

This exchange suggests that high Calvinism continued to exert an influence over Fuller. True, he said, "[T]he Lord is rich in mercy to all that call upon him," but, assuming this is where the conversation ended, there is no direct application of this truth to his father's personal situation and no explicit encouragement to trust in Christ. Probably Fuller found it easier to put his new principles into practice in the pulpit than one-to-one and doubtless his hesitation here was due in some degree to a natural reticence in speaking with his father. But this still falls rather short of what we might have expected at this stage of his career. Fuller did not find the break from high Calvinism easy.

Nevertheless, step-by-step his approach was changing. There are two particular indications of this. First of all, he was invited by the Baptist church at Kettering, Northamptonshire (known locally as the "Little Meeting") to consider their vacant pastorate. The initial invitation came at the end of 1779.[52] The church at Kettering was already committed to an evangelical Calvinism

---

[49] Diary entry for July 29, 1780, as recorded by Ryland, *Fuller*, 77. Those wishing to read Fuller's diaries can now do so in a critical edition, *The Diary of Andrew Fuller, 1780-81*, ed. Michael D. McMullen and Timothy D. Whelan (Berlin/Boston: Walter de Gruyter, 2016). The dairies Fuller kept at Soham are not extant, but the editors have drawn from the entries included by early biographers such as Ryland and Morris.

[50] Ryland, *Fuller*, 87.

[51] Ryland, *Fuller*, 88.

[52] Gunton Fuller, *Fuller*, 45.

and gave every impression they would be personally supportive (as part of this support they would be able to provide an adequate stipend). Fuller initially rebuffed the approach, feeling he was committed to Soham. The second indication of his developing ministry was that by the early 1780s there were conversions and baptisms and an increased number from Soham and surrounding areas coming to the Sunday services.[53] Yet, alongside this success, his problems at the church were growing.

As well as the opposition to his applied preaching, his perilous financial position continued to be a cause of grave concern. The issues with behaviour showed no signs of abating either. Soham's report for the May 1781 Association Meeting, ironically held at Kettering, included news of much discouragement due to the "disorderly walk" of a number of members.[54] In the "Narration," Fuller recorded that one member was "admonished" for "neglecting a church meeting, and being at an alehouse the chief part of the day." After the May Association matters got worse, and on September 9, 1781, a man was "excluded publickly, for Adultery!"[55] The exclamation mark in the "Narration" probably reflected the despair Fuller was feeling by this point. Diary entries for 1780 and 1781 reveal increasing unhappiness. A "continual heaviness lies upon me," he wrote.[56] Matters were coming to a head.

Leaving Soham

In the autumn of 1781, the Kettering church renewed their invitation to Fuller, asking him again to consider their pastorate. As he wrestled with the situation and agonised over what to do he experienced such "mental distress" that he became physically unwell. For a time he was unable to leave the house.[57] The Soham church knew of their pastor's unhappiness and also the approach from Kettering. They decided to refer the matter to Robert Robinson in Cambridge. Robinson advised Fuller to stay at Soham for at least another year. The Cambridge pastor further advised that Fuller's stipend should be raised to £26 per annum, something the Soham church had already agreed to in principle.[58] If

---

[53] Four were baptised in the period from May 1780 to May 1781. See Letter 6, May 1781 (Association at Kettering, Northamptonshire). See Ryland, *Fuller*, 44, for the increased numbers attending.

[54] Letter 6, May 1781.

[55] "Narration," 40.

[56] Ryland, *Fuller*, 45–47.

[57] Gunton Fuller, *Fuller*, 48.

[58] Ryland, *Fuller*, 51–52. Cf. Andrew Fuller, Letter to John Sutcliff, September 27, 1782, in F.G. Hastings, "Andrew Fuller and Ministerial Removals," *Baptist Quarterly* 8, no. 1 (January 1936): 12–13. The original letter is held in the Isaac Mann Collection, Yale University, New Haven, CT.

they failed to meet this financial condition, then Fuller would be free to leave at the end of the twelve-month period. Yet by now his financial position, precarious as it was, was not the primary issue. Indeed, it probably never had been.[59] A number of Fuller's friends, including Hall and Sutcliff, were disappointed with Robinson's advice.[60] Nevertheless, the Soham pastor wrote to the leading deacon at Kettering, Beeby Wallis, to tell the church there he could not respond positively to their invitation to go for a year's trial.[61] Ryland recorded that this was a "grievous disappointment" to the Kettering church.[62]

The matter was not at an end, however. It is unclear whether or not the Soham church kept its pledge to raise their pastor's income, but the other problems continued.[63] At last Fuller concluded he should leave, writing in the "Narration" on May 26, 1782, "my continuance [at Soham] would not be to my or their profit."[64] Yet, in the early summer of that year he was hesitating again. Finally, after an exchange of letters between himself and Kettering, he agreed to move. The final break was made on October 2, 1782, the date of Fuller's final Sunday as pastor at Soham.

Farewell sermons

As already noted, the extensive shorthand notes for the two farewell sermons have been largely deciphered and are now available for scholars to consult.[65] For his morning message, Fuller took Romans 8:28 as his text; in the evening he expounded Philippians 1:6. Four observations will be made concerning these important messages.

Firstly, the sermons' content and basic shape shows the impress of Full-

---

[59] Fuller himself made this clear. See "Narration," 48–49.

[60] For Hall's response, see Ryland, *Fuller*, 52. Cf. Robert Hall, Letter to Andrew Fuller, January 15, 1781 (Fuller Chapel Letters [Letters to Andrew Fuller], vol. 1 (1–34), vol. 2 (35–71), Fuller Baptist Church, Kettering), 1.1. Even early in 1781, Hall was hinting to his young friend he should move, although he expressed himself with great care. For Sutcliff's views, see Andrew Fuller, Letters to John Sutcliff, August 15, 1781 and September 27, 1782, in Hastings, "Andrew Fuller and Ministerial Removals," 13.

[61] Ryland, *Fuller*, 51–53.

[62] Ryland, *Fuller*, 54.

[63] Gunton Fuller, *Fuller*, 50.

[64] "Narration," 50.

[65] Stephen R. Holmes and Jonathan Woods, "Andrew Fuller's Soham Farewell Sermons: Context and Text," *Baptist Quarterly* 51, no. 1 (January 2020): 2–16. The text of the two messages is on pages 6–13. The authors estimate they are able to understand "with confidence" approximately 80% of Fuller's shorthand notes (Holmes and Woods, "Andrew Fuller's Soham Farewell Sermons," 5) in the five ms. books of sermon notes held by Bristol Baptist College. This breakthrough in reading Fuller's shorthand represents a considerable achievement.

er's evangelical biblicism. Fuller not only wrestled with his two chosen texts, he engaged with many others, making 39 biblical references over the course of the two sermons.[66] Further, his approach to preaching was textual rather than doctrinal, that is, he took a text and expounded it as opposed to stating a doctrine before defending and developing it, as tended to happen in Puritan sermons. In adopting his particular approach, Fuller was influenced by a work on homiletics by a seventeenth-century Huguenot pastor, Jean Claude, entitled *Essay on the Composition of a Sermon*. Claude's commendation of simplicity and "plain style" allied with the stress on Scripture exposition fitted well with the evangelical emphasis on the practical application of the Bible's message. Robert Robinson was an enthusiast for Claude, and published a translation of the *Essay* in 1778, with some added notes.[67] The Cambridge pastor had clearly been circulating his translation privately among other ministers some years before its publication.[68] There is little doubt that it was through Robinson that Fuller encountered Claude. Once again, we see how evangelical influences were mediated through friends and relevant literature.

Second, Fuller's Calvinism is on display in both messages. This paper has argued that a shift—indeed a seismic shift—occurred in Fuller's thinking and practice during his time at Soham. He rejected high Calvinism decisively. Yet the theology he now espoused was still Calvinistic. As Fuller expounded Romans 8:28, he reflected on God's providence and sovereignty. The "great ruler of heaven and earth sits at the helm of all affairs" and "keeps the world and all things in it in motion," he declared, using a typically homely illustration of a "well ordered working of a machine (a mill) which not only works but works together."[69] The exposition of Philippians 1:6 considered the final perseverance of the saints with reference to the "designs of God in eternal election to salvation through [the] Son."[70] Fuller had moved away from high Calvinism to espouse a more evangelical position. But this was still Calvinism. It should be no surprise that when Fuller offered a "statement of principles" at his induction service at Kettering on October 7, 1783, the essential tenets of Calvinistic

---

[66] As noted by Holmes and Woods, "Fuller's Farewell Sermons," 14.

[67] Jean Claude, *Essay on the Composition of a Sermon*, trans. and annotated Robert Robinson, 3rd ed. (London: Scollick, Wilson and Spence, 1788).

[68] Morris, *Fuller*, 69, states this was one of the first books the young pastor read following his induction. Fuller would later acknowledge his debt to Claude explicitly in his "Essay on the Composition of a Sermon..." published in an anonymously edited collection, *The Preacher, or Sketches of Original Sermons* (London: R. Baynes, 1822), 1:14–32 (see page 32). For a discussion, see Grant, *Fuller*, 79–87. Cf. Holmes and Woods, "Fuller's Farewell Sermons," 14–15.

[69] Holmes and Woods, "Fuller's Farewell Sermons," 7.

[70] Holmes and Woods, "Fuller's Farewell Sermons," 15.

thinking were all affirmed and Arminianism explicitly rejected.[71]

Third, Fuller's pastoral heart is evident in these two sermons. One searches in vain for anger or bitterness. In the morning he assured his people that God has "power" and "wisdom" enough to ensure all things work together, but "love … enough to make them answer one invariable end, the *good* of his people."[72] In the evening his closing point included the exhortation, "Take courage ye are engaged in Christ's cause. You fight in sure hope of victory."[73] His continued love for a church which had caused him significant grief shines through.

Fourth, Fuller urged that Christians should "be reconciled to trying disciplines." Why? Because of the dynamic that such "trying disciplines" are the very "means God uses to awaken, reclaim and carry on [his work]."[74] Fuller had experienced such "trying disciplines" at Soham. At the close of his pastorate, his account in the "Narration" was abruptly broken off, to be followed by a rather doleful entry in a different hand, "Bro. Fuller left the church and went to a place called Kettering."[75] The Soham Association letter for 1783 is more expressive, "surely Mr Fuller's leaving Soham was attended with many tears, some reflecting on themselves as having bin [sic] Instruments of Wo [sic]!"[76] The pastorate at Soham had been difficult indeed for Fuller. So, I do not believe it is fanciful to detect the note of personal experience in his comment that believers should be "reconciled" to such difficulties, treating them as "disciplines" through which God does his work. These painful disciplines provided the context in which Fuller's thinking and—our particular concern here—praxis were radically reshaped.

Conclusion
The period 1775–1782 saw a major shift in Fuller's practice of ministry, one that paralleled the sea-change in his theology. When he began his pastorate at Soham his praxis was congruent with high Calvinism, dubbed by Joseph Ivimey, not unfairly, as the "non-application, non-invitation scheme."[77] However,

---

[71] "Statement of Principles," as recorded by Ryland, *Fuller*, 65–68. The induction service only took place after the customary year's probation.

[72] Holmes and Woods, "Fuller's Farewell Sermons," 7.

[73] Holmes and Woods, "Fuller's Farewell Sermons," 13.

[74] Holmes and Woods, "Andrew Fuller's Soham Farewell Sermons," 13.

[75] "Narration," 50.

[76] Letter 8, 10 June 1783. As elsewhere in my quotations from MS material, I have retained the original spellings.

[77] Joseph Ivimey, *A History of the English Baptists* (London: B.J. Holdsworth, 1823), 3:272.

by the time he moved to Kettering, Fuller was preaching in an applied, invitational manner, urging his hearers—whoever they might be—to turn to Christ and trust him for salvation. This change in practice can be dated with confidence to December 1779, although this paper has argued that for at least a year after this date Fuller struggled to put his new-found principles into action. By the time he was inducted as pastor at Kettering, however, his commitment to Evangelical preaching was clear, unequivocal, and shaping his ministry week-by-week. There is arguably no more important development in the whole of Fuller's career than the one that took place in December 1779 at Soham.

Fuller would become arguably the foremost Baptist minister of his generation, a theologian whose works were hugely influential on both sides of the Atlantic, a widely-respected apologist and the founding secretary (in 1792) of the Baptist Missionary Society. He had come a long way from the "obscurity" of his upbringing and, indeed, of his first pastorate. What needs to be borne in mind by those who write about these later developments is the way the evangelical commitments which undergirded them were hammered out on the anvil of Fuller's "trying disciplines" at Soham.

"The poisonous influence of a corrupt Antinomian leaven": Caleb Evans' response to the Antinomianism of William Huntington

Casey G. McCall

Casey G. McCall serves as Lead Pastor of Ashland Avenue Baptist Church in Oldham County, KY. He is pursuing PhD studies in Church History at The Southern Baptist Theological Seminary. He can be reached at casey@ashlandoc.org.

The English Particular Baptists of the late eighteenth-century led an active denominational movement that challenged many long-held assumptions about the Christian life. In particular, church leaders such as Andrew Fuller (1754–1815), John Sutcliff (1752–1814), John Ryland, Jr. (1753–1825), and William Carey (1761–1834) sought, in a myriad of ways, to emphasize the value and necessity of human means into an ecclesial context smarting from the impact of High Calvinism.[1] This emphasis on human means is evident in the title to Carey's apology for cross-cultural missionary endeavors, *An Inquiry into the Obligation of Christians to Use Means for the Conversion of the Heathen*, published

---

[1] Peter Toon makes a distinction between between "High" Calvinism and "Hyper" Calvinism. He would label what I am describing here "Hyper" Calvinism. Nevertheless, he defines the doctrinal system as follows: "a system of theology ... framed to exalt the honour and glory of God and did at the expense of minimising the moral and spiritual responsibility of sinners to God. It placed excessive emphasis on the immanent acts of God—eternal justification, eternal adoption and the eternal covenant of grace ... It also made no distinction between the secret and the revealed will of God, and tried to deduce the duty of men from what it taught concerning the secret, eternal decrees of God." Peter Toon, *The Emergence of Hyper-Calvinism in English Nonconformity, 1689–1765* (Eugene, OR: Wipf and Stock, 1967), 144–145.

in 1792, the year before he set sail for Calcutta. This theological accent sparked the formation of the Baptist Missionary Society in 1792, was at the center of the Fuller-led debates over the "modern question," in which this group argued for the scriptural necessity of offering the gospel freely to all people, and led to an emphasis on social action that manifested itself notably in the fight to abolish slavery.[2] These thinkers represented a balanced Calvinism that maintained the absolute sovereignty of God, while simultaneously upholding the role of human action within divine purposes.

Caleb Evans (1737–1791) was an early proponent of this balanced Calvinism and undoubtedly impacted these younger leaders through his efforts in reorganizing the Bristol Baptist Academy and founding the Bristol Education Society in 1770.[3] Evans' perspective on the value of human means was clearly articulated in a sermon preached before the Bristol Education Society on August 16, 1775:

> When we pray for the advancement of this kingdom, if we are not willing to do all we can to advance it, our prayers cannot be genuine, they are hypocritical. When we pray that God would give us day by day our daily bread, we cannot be supposed to expect that he should give it us while we neglect the proper means of attaining it. And so when we pray that the kingdom of God may come, we are supposed to express a willingness to whatever God may enable us to do, as workers together with him, that it may come with greater and greater power and glory till it is brought to a state of perfection.[4]

Evans had little tolerance for a passive approach to the Christian life, even in the name of God's sovereignty. He refused to make divine sovereignty and human participation mutually exclusive categories. In Evans' mind, God's providential control did not lessen the need for human action; it provided the

---

[2] For an overview of the controversy surrounding the "modern question," see Jason C. Montgomery, "Benjamin Beddome and the Modern Question: The Witness of His Sermons," in *Glory to the Three Eternal: Tercentennial Essays on the Life and Writings of Benjamin Beddome (1718–1795)*, ed. Michael A.G. Haykin, Roy M. Paul, and Jeongmo Yoo, Monographs in Baptist History, vol. 13 (Eugene, OR: Pickwick Publications, 2019), 142–171. For a treatment of this group's active faith including their involvement in abolition efforts, see Michael A.G. Haykin, "'He Went About Doing Good': Eighteenth-Century Particular Baptists on the Necessity of Good Works," *American Theological Inquiry* 3, no. 1 (2010): 55–65.

[3] Kirk Wellum calls these efforts, "without doubt the most important contribution of Caleb Evans to the advancement of the kingdom of God" in his "Caleb Evans (1737–1791)" in *The British Particular Baptists, 1638–1910*, ed. Michael A.G. Haykin (Springfield, MO: Particular Baptist Press, 1998), 1:215.

[4] Caleb Evans, *The Kingdom of God. A Sermon, Preached in Broad-mead, Bristol, before the Bristol-Education-Society. August 16, 1775* (Bristol: W. Pine, T. Cadell, M. Ward, etc., 1775), 20–21.

grounds for it. This conviction eventually led Evans into conflict with William Huntington (1745–1813), a controversial High Calvinist who linked sanctification to divine election in such a way as to deny the need for believers to actively obey God's law, a doctrinal position known as Antinomianism.[5] Evans responded to Huntington by upholding the necessity of obedience to the law as a means of sanctification and as an essential outcome of genuine faith in Christ, a teaching that rooted him in the mainstream of the Reformed tradition and set a balanced tone for the Particular Baptists of the late eighteenth-century to follow.

William Huntington's Antinomianism

In every age of history, certain individuals have won notoriety through charisma and controversy, and William Huntington fulfilled that role in late eighteenth-century England. Converted out of a life of immorality, Huntington had an ecstatic spiritual experience and was shortly thereafter ordained to ministry in an Independent church. Robert W. Oliver notes that the isolated nature of his conversion experience led to a ministry that was largely independent of outside influences.[6] Huntington operated as a loner, even as his popularity grew. His church in London drew considerable crowds for the entirety of his thirty-year ministry, and many of those admirers were drawn from Particular Baptist churches.[7]

Antinomian strains can be traced all the way back to New Testament times. However, the practical Antinomianism of Huntington had a particularly English Puritan flavor that shared many similarities with seventeenth-century High Calvinist figures like Tobias Crisp and John Eaton.[8] The alarm surrounding Huntington arose more from his uncanny ability to popularize Antinomianism than from any unique doctrinal innovation. His numerous controversial writings and printed sermons coupled with his bombastic and charismatic style disseminated his teachings among Baptist churches enough to warrant a response from Caleb Evans and other Particular Baptist leaders.

Huntington's Antinomianism derived from a limited understanding of the use of the law of God within God's salvation economy coupled with a desire to

---

[5] For an extended treatment of the Particular Baptists' conflict with Huntington, see Robert W. Oliver, *History of the English Calvinistic Baptists, 1771–1892: From John Gill to C.H. Spurgeon* (Carlisle, PA: The Banner of Truth Trust, 2006), 112–145.

[6] Oliver, *History*, 120.

[7] Oliver, *History*, 121.

[8] For an overview of this history, see Curt D. Daniel, "Hyper-Calvinism and John Gill," (PhD diss., University of Edinburgh, 1983), 608–613. For a discussion of the historical link between High Calvinism and Antinomianism, see Toon, *Emergence of Hyper-Calvinism*, 49–69.

preserve God's absolute sovereignty and control within sanctification. The law of God, for Huntington, consisted of the decalogue along with all of the other teachings from Moses and the prophets that were derived from those ten commandments.[9] To him, God's law represented the holiness and righteousness of God and was, therefore, holy and righteous.[10] Huntington wrote, "The law cannot justify any man that is of the works of it, let him try his utmost: he is a debtor to do the whole commands of the law who works for life; and nothing less than a perfect, spiritual, and perpetual obedience will do to justify him who cleaves to it."[11] Therefore, the law could only condemn those outside of Christ. On these points, Huntington's detractors would have heartily agreed. The friction with the Particular Baptists did not result from Huntington's position on the revelatory nature of the law in showing God's righteous character or on the functional use of the law in condemning mankind and leading to Christ, but on his denial of a third use of the law for believers.

Presupposing that the law functions only to reveal and to condemn, Huntington could not allow for its use in the life of the Christian believer. Citing 1 Timothy 1:9 as proof, he wrote, "The law is not made for a righteous man, but for the lawless and disobedient."[12] On this point, Huntington was parting ways with John Calvin (1509–1564) and the mainstream of English Puritanism—a tradition that continued through John Gill (1697–1771) and the Particular Baptists. Calvin had maintained that the law "finds its place among believers in whose hearts the Spirit of God already lives and reigns" by continuing to teach them God's will, reaffirming his ways to their understanding.[13] For Calvin and those who followed, a distinction needed to be made between the law's negative use in condemning the unregenerate and the law's positive use in instructing the regenerate in the will of God. Gill, following this tradition, upheld the law's value for believers in specifying God's will, providing a rule of life, acting as a mirror in which to see one's own spiritual condition, and teaching the believer

---

[9] William Huntington, *The Law Established by the Faith of Christ. A Sermon, Preached at Providence Chapel, On the First Day of January, 1786* (London: Denew and Grant, 1786), 10.

[10] Huntington, *Law Established*, 11.

[11] Huntington, *Law Established*, 25.

[12] William Huntington, *The Bond Child Brought to the Test; and His Use of the Letter Considered* (London, 1789), 9.

[13] John Calvin, *Institutes of the Christian Religion* 2.7.12, The Library of Christian Classics 20, ed. John T. McNeill and trans. Ford Lewis Battles (Louisville, KY: Westminster John Knox, 1960), 1:360. Calvin's position later came to be formalized within the Reformed tradition as the "three uses of the law." Under this scheme, the law 1) acts as a mirror of God's righteousness and gives knowledge of sin; 2) restrains sin in the civic realm; and 3) guides the regenerate to live in obedience.

to prize the righteousness of Christ.[14] Both Calvin's *Institutes* and Gill's *Body of Doctrinal Divinity* were read at Evans' Bristol Education Society.[15] Huntington, on the other hand, absolutized Paul's teaching in Romans concerning the law's role in justification and refused to acknowledge a distinction between the law working on the unregenerate and the law working on the regenerate. For him, the law only condemned, no matter the spiritual state of the person, which, in his mind, left his opponents with two choices: either join him as a "rank Antinomian," thus agreeing with Paul, or assume the title of "ministers of the letter."[16]

If the law is incapable of guiding the believer in the ways of God, by what rule is the believer to live? Huntington answered this question by turning to faith. Drawing a sharp distinction between faith and the law, he wrote, "Thus faith appears to be the believer's rule of life, according to the will of God in Christ Jesus; and the letter of the law is the bond-children's rule of life."[17] The law, he wrote, based on Jeremiah 31:33, had been established in the heart of every authentic child of God through faith in Christ.[18] Huntington's understanding of the New Covenant omitted the need for the believer to reference the moral law and, according to Oliver, encouraged believers to look to experience rather than to God's written revelation.[19] Insisting on his distinction between the external law that only condemns and the internal law that has been written on the heart, Huntington wrote, "Does not the Scripture say that he walks by faith, and lives by faith, and works by faith? On which account his obedience is called the obedience of faith, his life the life of faith, and his works the works of faith."[20] For him, the possibility of the law guiding the life of faith was not feasible; the law and faith had to represent contrary approaches to God.

Aside from denying any positive function of the law of God in the life of the believer, Huntington was also driven by a deep concern to maintain God's sovereignty in all of life, including sanctification. His emphasis on faith, noted above, allowed him to articulate a vision for the Christian life in which man

---

[14] John Gill, *A Body of Doctrinal Divinity; Or, A System of Evangelical Truths, Deduced from the Sacred Scriptures* (London: George Keith, 1769), 2:592.

[15] *An Alphabetical Catalogue of All the Books in the Library, Belonging to the Bristol Education Society* (Bristol: W. Pine and Son, 1795). I am grateful to Alex C. Tibbott for showing me this catalogue.

[16] Huntington, *Bond Child*, 24.

[17] William Huntington, *A Rule and a Riddle; or, An Everlasting Task for Blind Watchmen and Old Women. In a Letter to a Friend* (London: T. Bensley, 1788), 14.

[18] Huntington, *Law Established*, 41.

[19] Oliver, *History*, 126.

[20] Huntington, *Bond Child*, 21.

was primarily passive. He wrote, "There are five things, reader, which will make thee and me fruitful, and acceptable … and that is—a union with the true living Vine; a confidence in the blood and righteousness of the Saviour; the dominion of grace reigning through righteousness; the promise of God that we shall bring forth fruit in old age; and the certainty of the Holy Ghost abiding with us forever."[21] While no evangelical contemporary would have denied the importance of these truths, Huntington's arrangement so emphasized God's role in sanctification that very little emphasis was given to man's responsibility to respond.

In classic High Calvinist fashion, Huntington so emphasized God's will of decree that God's moral will, wherein God reveals his guiding desire for humanity, was rendered obsolete. For Huntington, God's sovereign will of purpose *was* the believer's rule of life. He wrote, "There is one rule … and that rule is, the sovereign, absolute, and uncontroulable will of God in Christ Jesus. *God worketh all things after the counsel of his own will* … consequently all things will lay straight with that rule; and that we shall find if we bring them there."[22] Advancement in the Christian life depended solely upon continuing to trust God to work his sovereign will. Huntington emphasized sanctification as an instantaneous result of union with Christ, writing, "By virtue of their union with him [saints] have sanctification in him, and are sanctified by him."[23]

Furthermore, Huntington associated union with Christ, not with the moment in time of human faith, but with God's eternal decree: "The *bond of all perfectness* is not our faith in God, but God's eternal love to us. The former is not the efficient cause, but the effect, of the latter."[24] An emphasis on progressive sanctification is entirely lacking in his writings because sanctification, in his scheme, was completed at the same time as justification and union with Christ—at the moment of God's eternal decree of election.[25] The elected believer, therefore, experiences holiness, not by obeying God's law, but by "enjoying union and communion with Christ."[26] Holiness, according to Huntington, was not a yet-to-be-attained future goal, but an already-established-state to be en-

---

[21] Huntington, *Bond Child*, 40.

[22] Huntington, *Law Established*, 59.

[23] William Huntington, *The Music and Odours of Saints. A Sermon, Preached at Providence Chapel, Sept. 2, 1787* (London: G. Terry, 1788), 81.

[24] William Huntington, *The Broken Cistern, and the Springing Well: Or, The Difference Between Head Notions, and Heart Religion, Vain Jangling, and Sound Doctrine. Addressed to the Rev. John Ryland, Senior, at Enfield*, 2nd ed. (London: T. Bensley, 1800), 23.

[25] Huntington, *Broken Cistern*, 32.

[26] Huntington, *Broken Cistern*, 30.

joyed through communion with the God who decreed it.

The subtlety of Huntington's scheme needs to be noted. He did not propagate teachings that the contemporary reader would have found heretical. In fact, much of what he wrote resonated in tone with the apostle Paul's writings, and he often put himself in the place of Paul, identifying his opponents with the voices of Paul's opponents.[27] He also published many works and covered the same themes from varying angles and often in response to opponents, making it difficult to locate precision and consistency in his writings. Nevertheless, by the last decade of the eighteenth-century, the British Particular Baptists had identified Huntington's Antinomianism as a threat to their churches. In spite of his claim to be representing the teachings of Paul, they concluded that his theology was out of balance.

Caleb Evans' affirmation of the law
When Caleb Evans presented his circular letter to the Western Association's annual meeting at Horsley, Gloucestershire, in 1789, he did not mention the name "William Huntington." He wrote to combat what he called the "poisonous influence of a corrupt Antinomian leaven," which he considered particularly dangerous due to Antinomianism's ability to masquerade under the guise of genuine grace. Antinomianism, he maintained, "pretends to exalt the free and sovereign grace of God, to reduce the creature to nothing, and to make God and Christ all in all."[28] Nevertheless, Huntington interpreted the letter as a direct attack and published a lengthy personal response.[29] The published correspondence between the two men ended there with Evans refusing to engage the noted controversialist publicly.[30] The circular letter, however, while certainly addressing Antinomianism more directly by name, did not contain anything theologically that Evans had not already promoted through his other published writings and sermons.

Antinomianism was already in Evans' view in 1779, ten years before his circular letter and five years prior to the first of Huntington's Antinomian publications, when Evans published an associational sermon entitled, *The Law Established by the Gospel*. In the advertisement, Evans noted that friends request-

---

[27] See, for example, Huntington, *Law Established*, 3ff.

[28] *Circular Letter of the Western Association* (1789), 6.

[29] William Huntington, *A Letter to the Rev. Caleb Evans, M.A. Master of the Seminary at Bristol. Containing a Few Remarks on a Circular Letter Drawn Up by Him*, 2nd ed. (London: T. Bensley, 1798).

[30] Stephen Albert Swaine, *Faithful Men; or, Memorials of Bristol Baptist College, and Some of Its Most Distinguished Alumni* (London: Alexander and Shepheard, 1884), 174. Swaine wrote, "Apparently, however, the doctor disdained to enter into controversy with Mr. Huntington, and no one acquainted with the style of controversial writing adopted by the 'saved sinner' will express surprise" (Swaine, *Faithful Men*, 174).

ed its publication in response "to that unjust charge against the distinguishing doctrines of the gospel, that they tend to loosen our obligations to personal holiness, and secretly countenance licentiousness."[31] In the sermon Evans chose the latter part of Romans 3:31 for his text, which states simply, "We establish the law." He began the sermon by noting that "it would be the strongest objection that could possibly be formed against the glorious gospel, were it really true that it makes void the law."[32] Distinguishing the moral law from the ceremonial law, Evans insisted that Christ had not cancelled it, but "republished" it when he gave the two greatest commandments to love God and love neighbor in Matthew 22:37–40.[33]

Evans' positions on the law's function in condemning sinners and its inability to bring life and salvation were essentially identical to those of Huntington. Evans, however, maintained the continued necessity of the law as a rule for Spirit-indwelt believers in Christ. He observed from his text that Paul considered the objection that the gospel voids the law "the fullest confutation … that could be offered."[34] Paul, Evans maintained, "was no Antinomian, either in principle or practice."[35] The gospel, according to Evans, not only did not void the law, it actually established both its "supreme dignity and authority" and its importance as a rule of life, providing "the believer with the strongest motives to obedience which can be offered to the human mind."[36] To Evans, the awful sufferings that Christ endured only magnified the dignity of the law, because those sufferings were necessary in order to meet the law's demands.[37] The true recipient of God's pardoning love can only approach God's law with "cheerful glad obedience."[38]

This theme was still on Evans' mind in October of the same year when he preached a funeral sermon for a certain Dr. Joseph Mason. In this sermon, after articulating clearly the law's inability to justify a sinner and the necessity of the imputed righteousness of Christ by faith, Evans wrote:

---

[31] Caleb Evans, *The Law Established by the Gospel. A Sermon, Preached Before the Ministers and Messengers, of the Baptist Western Association, Assembled at Exon, June 3, 1779* (Bristol: W. Pine, 1779), iii.

[32] Evans, *Law Established*, 5.

[33] Evans, *Law Established*, 6–7.

[34] Evans, *Law Established*, 15.

[35] Evans, *Law Established*, 16.

[36] Evans, *Law Established*, 17–18.

[37] Evans, *Law Established*, 20.

[38] Evans, *Law Established*, 26.

But as the very reason of the sinner's being justified by the perfect righteousness of Christ and not by his own imperfect righteousness, is to magnify the law and make it honorable, and the more deeply to impress us with a sense of the nature and desert of sin, and the infinite importance of holiness; so we can never suppose that we are led to the righteousness of Christ for justification to teach us to neglect or be indifferent about personal righteousness, but rather to engage us by motives of the most awful and yet attractive nature, the more strongly to love and delight in it; and to render a known and deliberate deviation from it, I had almost said impossible.[39]

Evans often used funeral sermons to reaffirm the connection between real gospel faith and a life of holiness. Undoubtedly, Evans sought to take advantage of the unique opportunities provided by funerals to preach to more diverse audiences and to press the nature of genuine faith to the more tender consciences of those who gathered to mourn. In one such sermon in 1790, he made the connection between gospel faith and practical holiness by insisting that the gospel "is a doctrine according to godliness" and "does not lead to licentiousness but constrains to holiness."[40]

Clearly, the circular letter of 1789 represented the same position that Evans had maintained throughout the entirety of his ministry, a position consistent with that of Calvin, Gill, and the Reformed tradition. Antinomianism, however, was not his only target in this address to the Western Association. He also spoke to the legalists, or those who sought holiness while neglecting the gospel of grace, pointing out the futility of such efforts. Such people, he said, "might as well seek grapes from thorns, or figs from thistles," for no fruit will come unless the doctrines of the gospel are "explained, understood, and applied to your hearts by the good Spirit of God."[41] After this short warning and another brief word against Socinianism, Evans spent the bulk of the letter attacking the subtle threat of Antinomianism.

Roger Hayden has pointed out that the High Calvinists often evaded the clear teaching of Scripture in favor of doctrinal presuppositions derived from their High Calvinist system.[42] Evans not only sought to level the erroneous position of the Antinomians on the law, but he also took aim at the High Calvinist

---

[39] Caleb Evans, *The Hope of the Righteous in Death* (Bristol: W. Pine, 1780), 12–13.

[40] Caleb Evans, *The Faithful Servant Crowned* (Bristol: William Pine, 1790), 12.

[41] *Circular Letter*, 3–4.

[42] Roger Hayden, *Continuity and Change: Evangelical Calvinism Among Eighteenth-Century Baptist Ministers Trained at Bristol Academy, 1690–1791* (Chipping Norton, Oxfordshire: Baptist Historical Society, 2006), 185.

system which undergirded it. He recognized the way in which the systematic desire to protect God's absolute sovereignty led to a tendency to ignore other clear teachings in Scripture and resulted in practical Antinomianism. He critiqued the position that so emphasized God's eternal decrees in marking the elect that "the sins of believers are therefore no evidence at all of their being interested in the love of God."[43] The evidence, he maintained, of God's electing love is always manifested in holiness of one's life.

Evans also documented the tendency among this group to confuse the permissive will of God with God's preceptive will, and with this claim, he was responding specifically to an argument made by Huntington, though he did not name him. In Huntington's sermon, *The Law Established by the Faith of Christ*, he had argued that Peter's betrayal of Jesus was orchestrated by the sovereign will of God. His larger point was that God's sovereign will, and not the moral law, was the believer's chief rule of life.[44] In other words, Huntington believed that Peter was obeying God even as he violated God's revealed will. Evans maintained that Huntington here was allowing his system to negate the nuances between God's will of decree and God's moral will. It was ludicrous to him to think that "Peter had been yielding as much obedience in cursing and swearing and denying his Lord, as ever he did when performing an act of obedience to any precept of the moral law."[45] It was even more preposterous to Evans that Antinomians like Huntington were being lifted up as "the only preachers of the pure gospel."[46]

Huntington's response and later controversy
As noted above, Huntington interpreted Evans' circular letter as a direct attack and responded with a 130-page letter to Evans, reaffirming his position regarding the law of God. In fact, Huntington used this tract to double down on some of the most controversial aspects of his teaching. Further conflating God's will of decree with God's moral will and inculcating a passive approach to sanctification, he insisted, based on Ephesians 2:10, that "good works do not spring from God's will of commandments, but from his will of purpose."[47] Therefore, Huntington maintained that man was not the active agent in good works, but God. He discouraged any conception of sanctification as a process and associated sanctification as a progressive work with Sarah's "bond-woman." To stress

---

[43] *Circular Letter*, 8.

[44] Huntington, *Law Established*, 62.

[45] *Circular Letter*, 10.

[46] *Circular Letter*, 10.

[47] Huntington, *Letter*, 89.

progressive sanctification, according to Huntington, was "to forward the business by the works of the flesh, instead of lying passive to be worked on."[48] In all matters related to salvation and the Christian life, God's activity rendered human recipients passive.

Caleb Evans died in 1791, a mere two years after the publication of his circular letter, but the conflicts between Huntington and the Particular Baptists continued. Huntington, in fact, attributed Evans' death to God's judgment for Evans' opposition to Huntington's doctrine.[49] Subsequently, John Ryland, Jr., Andrew Fuller, and John Rippon (1751–1836) all came under the attack of Huntington's pen.[50] In 1818, Ryland, Jr., reflecting back on his life and ministry, remarked that "had it pleased God to remove me from this world at any period between the year 1791 and the death of this man, no doubt he would have added my name to the list of those who were struck dead for not receiving him."

Conclusion

Caleb Evans' defense of the law as a rule of life for the believer in Christ situates him within the mainstream Reformed tradition and affirms his position as a key theological tone-setter among late eighteenth-century Particular Baptists. His insistence on the connection between faith and glad obedience to God's law represents well the balanced Calvinism that came to characterize the English Particular Baptists of that era. While continuing to emphasize God's sovereignty in all of life, Evans refused to negate the means through which God accomplishes his decrees on earth. In William Huntington's Antinomianism, Evans saw a dangerous system that failed to account for the fullness of what God had revealed regarding sanctification. He set the tone for his tradition's theological revolt against passivity, and that revolt would continue through the various efforts of the Particular Baptists for several decades after his death.

---

[48] Huntington, *Letter*, 31–32.

[49] Oliver, *History*, 139.

[50] Oliver, *History*, 138.

Texts & documents

"Extracts from six letters written by Benjamin Beddome in 1759 and 1760"

ed. and annotated Gary Brady

Gary Brady, ThM, has been pastor of Childs Hill Baptist Church, London, since 1983.

Following his death, Particular Baptist minister Benjamin Beddome (1718–1795) continued to have an impact through his writings. In his lifetime, he had published only one book (*A Scriptural Exposition of the Baptist Catechism*) but in 1817 a large collection of hymns appeared and between 1807 and 1820 a goodly number of his sermons were printed in a series of eight slim volumes (*Short discourses adapted to village worship or the devotion of the family*). The sermons went through several editions and in 1835 were reissued in a larger combined format with a fresh volume of 67 more sermons.

A volume of letters has never appeared although a number of Beddome's letters are extant. In 1800, *The Evangelical Magazine* featured extracts from six letters written in 1759 and 1760. At the time that he wrote these letters Beddome was in his early forties. The last two contain hymns. Interestingly, unlike the other letters, these two were penned on a Saturday and probably contain the hymn that Beddome had composed that week and that would be sung the next day.[1]

The Evangelical Magazine was a Calvinistic periodical and was aimed at

---

[1] A letter exists in the Angus Library written to Richard Hall on a Saturday afternoon containing a hymn. There Beddome explicitly states it has been written for the next day.

both Nonconformists and members of the Established Church. It began in 1793, merging with *The Missionary Chronicle* in 1812. The founding editor was Anglican clergyman John Eyre (1754–1803). The letters appear in the April to September editions of 1800. They were provided by someone with the initials S.C., who obtained them from a relative of Beddome's. Most likely S.C. would be the Luton-born Baptist preacher Samuel Chase but his dates are usually given as 1787–1863 making him rather young to be doing this sort of thing. However, he was baptised by John Ryland at the Broadmead Church in Bristol when only 13 and is said to have studied at Bristol Baptist Academy around 1802 and 1803. If these tentative dates are revised down a little, it is no surprise to find a student in Bristol, where Beddome had also studied, had grown up, and still had relatives, as the conduit for these letters. An obituary for Chase's mother appeared in *The Evangelical Magazine* for 1798.

It is not possible to identify the recipient of the letters. In 1760 Beddome's two sisters, Mary and Martha, still lived in Bristol. One of the letters uses the term cousin so it is unlikely to be a sibling. Mary's daughter Mary Brain (1744–1819) would have been a teenager in 1760 and could possibly be the one who received and shared the letters. Beddome's cousins, the children of his mother and father's siblings, may have been as many as five.

Note

The first letter is prefaced by: "The following original letter of that excellent and ingenious man, the late Rev. B. Beddome, pastor of the Baptist Church at Bourton on the water, having lately been put into my hands by one of his relations to whom it was addressed; I obtained leave to make an extract, which you are at liberty to insert in the Evangelical Magazine, if it pleases you as well as it has done your correspondent. S C."

Letter 1

Bourton, July 23, 1759

I lament that my conversation when you were at Bourton was not more instructive. Alas! I often think of the words of one of the first Reformers: "Old Adam is too cunning for Melanchthon."[2] If my preaching has been blessed to others, if it was so in the least measure to you, not the preacher, but God must have the glory. Whatever I hear from others, I see, I feel, enough in myself to

---

[2] The quotation is from Philip Melanchthon (1497–1560) himself. In his youthful zeal Melanchthon had left the university lecture hall for the squares of Wittenberg to evangelise. On his return, his mentor Luther asked how he had got on, eliciting the rueful reply. "Old Adam was too hard for young Melancthon [sic]." See Francis Augustus Cox, *The Life of Philip Melancthon* [sic], 2nd ed. (London: Gale and Fenner; Edinburgh: Oliphant, Waugh, and Innes, 1817), 130.

keep me humble. May your good wishes in your letter be continually turned into fervent prayers to God, in my behalf: for I may say of the things wished, as David does of the well-ordered covenant, they contain all my salvation, and are all my desire; and I return them by wishing you all needful supplies of grace here, and a well-grounded soul-enlivening hope of glory hereafter—O may we be more and more prepared for that state where all the endearments of friendship will be felt, without those unhappy mixtures which embitter all its sweets upon earth.

Thus prays, yours, etc. BB

Letter 2

October 18, 1759

Dear Cousin,

Though the motions of the wheels of Providence are rough and intricate, nay, though they are retrograde, and sometimes seem to go back, yet there are eyes within and without,[3] and I doubt not but all thing are ordered by an infinitely wise God for your good and advantage. I hope you have found the school of affliction to be the school of Christ, and that you can say with David, in very faithfulness thou hast afflicted me.

In your last you told me of a promise that had been sweet to you: by that God was by preparing you for the sorrowful scene that followed. He allured you, and brought you into the wilderness, and I trust he has there spoken comfortably to you.[4] The bitter cup is sometimes as necessary as the cordial draught; and when God teaches us, as Gideon did the men of Succoth, by the briars and thorns of the wilderness, his lessons often often make the deepest impression.[5] I shall be heartily glad to hear of the perfect restoration of your health and above all, of your spiritual welfare, I am, etc.

BB

---

[3] An allusion to Revelation 4:8 and to Ezekiel 1 and 10.

[4] An allusion to Hosea 2:14.

[5] See Judges 8.

Letter 3

May 19, 1760

_____ When you lent Sister H_____ Mr Thomas's diary,[6] she promised not to let it go from her, and she scrupulously fulfilled her promise, so that I could not get a sight of it. Since that I borrowed it of Mr S[7] and read it with great delight, and indeed amazement, that a person about the age of twelve or thirteen should be able to write with such propriety.

"Peace!—Praise! I have peace." That there is peace procured, though we should have no personal interest in it, is matter of praise. That we have peace, peace with God, peace within, that peace that passeth all understanding, and which the world cannot give nor take away, lays a foundation for loftier praises still; and peace in a dying hour should raise our notes to the highest pitch: then one dram of true peace is worth all the world; the one we leave behind us, the other we take with us. "The work of righteousness shall be peace, and the effect of righteousness quietness and of assurance for ever." That we might often meet at the throne of grace in this world, remembering each other there, and finally meet before the throne of glory above, is the earnest desire and I would hope, fervent prayer of

Yours affectionately BB.

Letter 4

July 17, 1760

I am obliged to you for your last kind letter and heartily wish I could answer it with the same humble, savoury and spiritual frame with which you seem to have written it but this is what I want, and sometimes fear I never shall attain, to have my pen, my tongue, proclaim aloud the Lord Jesus Christ, the wonders

---

[6] The minister referred to is Timothy Thomas (c.1700–1720), pastor for a brief period of time at Pershore. Beddome quotes Thomas' dying words at the beginning of his final paragraph. Thomas was preceded in the Pershore pastorate by his father, also Timothy Thomas, pastor from 1696/7 until his death in 1716. Thomas, Sr. and his wife Anne were Welsh. She tried to procure Philip Doddridge (1702–1751) as pastor of the open communion church, following her son's death. By 1760 John Ash was the pastor (he came in 1746). Thomas, Jr. died prematurely, only three years into the pastorate and no more than 21 years of age. His personality continued to speak in his diary and letters, which, a generation later, were handed by his sister to Thomas Gibbons (1720–1785), minister of the Independent Church at Haberdashers Hall, London, who in 1752 published them anonymously as *The Hidden Life of a Christian*. It is interesting that the young man's eager, devout spirit evidently made an instant appeal to those caught up in the Evangelical Revival (a second edition was soon called for and it was translated into Welsh) even though he wrote in the years 1710–1720, when religion in England is often supposed to have been at a low ebb.

[7] A single letter is not enough to make an identification. Was it the London based Seventh-day Baptist Samuel Stennett (1727–1795)?

of his dying love and riches of his sovereign grace.

I want more of that poverty of spirit whereby a Christian sees his own sin and misery, and yet hopes in God's mercy; performs duties, and yet does not trust in them; assigns all his failings to himself, and all his excellencies to Jesus Christ: but why should I multiply particulars?

In all the lives that I have read and they are not a few, I never met with so wanting, and yet so undeserving a creature as myself. The Lord lead me to the fulness of Jesus Christ, not to make use of him as a man does of his deeds, bonds, and other securities for money, which he looks upon, perhaps, once in a long season, to see whether they are safe, and then takes no further thought about them; but I would live upon Jesus Christ as a man does upon his daily bread. I am satisfied that religion will never flourish in my soul till I am enabled so to do for all religion begins in the knowledge of him, thrives by communion with him and is compleated [sic] in the enjoyment of him. Christ is the Christian's All. Sometimes I think I can say as the Church—Isa. 26:18 "*Yea in the way of thy judgments, etc*" but I want to say as she does—Cantic. 3:4 *"It was but a little that I passed, etc."* Yet will I wait God's time, for that is best, and the longer the mercy is delayed the more welcome will it be when it comes. Besides, we are told the Lord is good to them who wait for him, to the soul which seeketh him. May you know but little of the distresses I sometimes feel and much of the comforts for which I long and wait.

BB

Letter 5

September 27, 1760

With respect to your spiritual concerns, what shall I say? Your soul is in the best hand; your most important interests are lodged with the great Redeemer; to him the Father hath committed them; to him you have been enabled, by divine grace, to commit them; and he will be faithful to his trust. A sense of an interest is desirable, but there may be an interest where there is not a sense of it. I wish I had your evidences. This I can say, that I mourn—I look upwards. All that is dark and distressing in your letter, I feel; all that is otherwise, I want.

> O God all-holy and all-wise,
> Open my heart, open my eyes;
> Reveal thyself, reveal thy Son,
> And make thy great salvation known.

As once of old, so now proclaim
Thy wond'rous love, thy gracious name;
To me thy pard'ning mercy show,
And spread the joys of heav'n below.

My tuneful voice I then will raise,
And all my powers shall tune thy praise;
I'll in thy church thy works declare,
And celebrate thy glories there.

It has been a consolatory [sic] thought to me, that God is more glorified in the salvation of one soul through Christ, than in the destruction of a whole world. O for a savory spirit, an evangelical temper of mind! Dear friend, pray for me, that while I want I may experience and then you shall meet with the same return from your unworthy, though affectionate friend,

BB

Letter 6

December 13, 1760

'Tis sin disorders all my frame,
Nor can this world afford me rest;
The law does nothing but condemn,
In Christ alone can I be blest.

'Tis his grace, 'tis in his blood,
I sweet refreshment hope to find;
His blood can cleanse my crimson guilt,
His grace can bow my stubborn mind.

Prostrate beneath his feet I wait,
For a kind look, or quick'nng word;
Shine in on my distressed soul
My King, my Saviour, and my Lord.[8]

Here you have the language of my lips, the language of my pen, and I trust the

---

[8] This hymn appears at the close of a published sermon on Jeremiah 13:27 with the title *Necessity of Holiness*. See the eighth sermon in *Twenty Short Discourses, Adapted to Village Worship, or The Devotions of the Family*, 2nd ed. (Dunstable: J.W. Morris, 1807), 55.

language of my heart. Though I find it hard to pray to God, and harder still to wait for God. "I waited patiently for the Lord," says David.[9] O that is not as easy a thing as some may account it. We are apt to kick against the pricks,[10] to rebel under the smarting rod, and accuse God of severity, when he does not immediately bestow the promised and expected blessings. I have much reason to complain of a stubborn and untractable heart, an unsubmissive temper of mind.

Yours, etc BB

---

[9] Psalm 40:1.

[10] See Acts 26:14.

On being missional—a letter of Andrew Fuller to George Charles Smith[1]

ed. Michael A.G. Haykin

Michael A.G. Haykin is Chair and Professor of Church History and Director, The Andrew Fuller Center for Baptist Studies at The Southern Baptist Theological Seminary, Louisville, Kentucky.

Introduction

George Charles Smith (1782–1863) had a noteworthy ministry among sailors and soldiers, but he was quite eccentric. He once referred to himself as "George Charles Smith BBU," that is, "George Charles Smith Burning Bush Unconsumed"![2] Around 1810 he sought Andrew Fuller's advice on the formation of a society devoted to the evangelization of seamen. Fuller's reply below is a fabulous distillation of his thinking about how to do missions. Not surprisingly, in the course of the nineteenth-century British institutionalization of the missionary endeavour, Fuller's advice fell out of favour.

---

[1] This letter can be found in [George Charles Smith,] "First Naval Mission, Andrew Fuller, Isaiah Birt, etc.," *The Mariners' Church Gospel Temperance Soldiers & Sailors' Magazine* [Supplement], 28, no.12 (December, 1847): 4–7. I am extremely thankful to Rev. Jared Skinner, a doctoral student at Southern Seminary, for drawing my attention to this letter. It will appear in a forthcoming volume: Michael A.G. Haykin, *Reading Andrew Fuller* (Peterborough, ON: H&E Publishing).

[2] "George Charles (Bo'sun) Smith 1782–1863," *St. George-in-the-East* (http://www.stgitehistory.org.uk/media/bosunsmith.html; accessed August 14, 2020). For his life, see Roald Kverndal, *George Charles Smith of Penzance: From Nelson Sailor to Mission Pioneer* (Littleton, CO: William Carey Library, 2012). See also Richard Blake, *Evangelicals in the Royal Navy 1775–1815: Blue Lights & Psalm-Singers* (Woodbridge, Suffolk: The Boydell Press, 2008), 232–237.

Andrew Fuller, Letter to George Charles Smith

Kettering, January 1, 1811

My dear Brother Smith:
The regard you have for the poor sailors endeared you to me. Indeed, I consider it as put into your heart by the Lord, and as betokening designs of mercy. It was probably for this purpose that Providence placed you at sea in your earlier days. I give full credit to your account of the deplorable state of the navy, in a moral and religious view. The only question is, what are the best practicable means of ameliorating it! From the first mention of a society, I was struck with apprehension. Brother Greatheed was convinced that unless we could obtain authority sanctioning a person's going on board to distribute tracts, Bibles, etc. we could do nothing even were we to form a society.[3] But such an authority I am persuaded cannot be obtained; it may be done by connivance, just as we have obtained footing in India, but no otherwise. To form a society for the express purpose would defeat the end.

Being less acquainted with naval matters than those who reside at our principal sea-ports, I wrote to Mr. Birt as follows: "I should expect such a society would raise a flame of persecution against the poor men from their officers; and, therefore, everything that is done, should be done in a still and quiet way, merely by individuals, who, whatever understanding they may have with each other, should not exist as a body. We know there is no part of the community so little at liberty as the army and navy; but the law allows them to write and receive letters from individuals on shore. This, therefore, is the door that is open; and if we go beyond it, may not this door some way be contrived to shut upon us? You, living at a sea-port, may be better able to give an opinion on this question than many others; I will, therefore, thank you for it."[4] To this I have received an answer, as follows: "Your objections to a nautical society, and your plan of doing everything merely by individuals, meet my most perfect approbation. The navy and army are servants. Suppose a society formed to promote religion among the king's household servants, or servants in gentlemen's families, would it not be a high offence, and so defeat the end? We call it religion, but they would call it Methodism,[5] and set themselves against it; when, if only

---

[3] Samuel Greatheed (1759–1823) was the rector at Bishops Hull, Somerset.

[4] Isaiah Birt (1758–1837) was the pastor of the Baptist church in Devonport. The Birmingham Congregationalist John Angell James (1785–1859) once said of him that he was "no ordinary man. His preaching was richly evangelical ... [and his] gift in prayer was extraordinary." Cited S. Pearce Carey, *Samuel Pearce, M.A., The Baptist Brainerd* [London: The Carey Press, 1913]), 59.

[5] I.e., fanaticism.

conducted by individuals, in a still way, the gospel might penetrate even to king's palaces."

I think I stated to brother Greatheed in my last, that I had written to William Wilberforce, Esq., M.P.,[6] copying the greater part of the letters from Hubback and Tooly,[7] and a part of Mr. Greatheed's to me, containing his proposals, and submitting a few questions upon them; to this I have received the following answers: "December 24th, 1810. I have received your most interesting letter, and will myself consider and consult with some friends as to the best course to be pursued for the attainment of the object, which must be dear to all who are interested for religion, and even for religious liberty." "December 25th. I am entirely of opinion, that if we were to form a society expressly for the purpose of carrying into effect the excellent suggestion of Mr. Greatheed, (for whom, having had the pleasure of being introduced to him last summer, I need not say I feel a real esteem and regard) it would excite so much alarm as entirely to defeat the object. I doubt whether there be any better mode of proceeding than that of finding out some confidential and unexceptionable person at each of the great sea-ports, who might be supplied with tracts [and Bibles] by the three societies you mention, and by whom a communication might be obtained with the ships of war. But we must proceed very cautiously and circumspectly; and it is highly important that in all your communications on this subject you should enjoin the strictest secrecy. Perhaps it may be desirable to lose no time in endeavoring to find persons of the above description at the different sea-ports."

You allow that much noise would be made by the formation of a new society, and that considerable opposition might be expected, but think it would meet with so many advocates, and be an object so popular in the general, that nothing would ultimately defeat the grand object. That it might be popular, and meet with many advocates among religious people, I allow: I should not reckon, however, on universal approbation even there; for though it would not be a party business, yet there is so much of party spirit among religious people, that whoever took the lead, they would be suspected by others; and while some were zealous advocates, others would give a suspicious colouring to the whole. But allowing the utmost of your expectations, yet the whole body of religious people in the land are as nothing in comparison of the irreligious. Irreligious churchmen, irreligious Dissenters, and, what are more numerous that all others put together, irreligious absenters, form the bulk of the nation. This last description of men, I mean those who attend no worship in ordinary, abound in the legislature, and in all public offices, civil, military, or naval, and

---

[6] William Wilberforce (1759–1833), the Evangelical abolitionist.

[7] In a footnote, Fuller noted that these were the names of two "seamen, in different ships of war, who corresponded with me."

are always ready to use their utmost influence against religion, which they hate with a mortal hatred.

I remember, as may also brother Greatheed, that about the year 1787, when there were meetings all over the country for an application to Parliament for the repeal of the Corporation and Test Acts,[8] great expectations were entertained from the popularity of the measure, and the advocates we should have in Parliament—as if reason were to prevail over interest. Some were so sanguine, if I remember right, as to intimate that Parliament dare not refuse us. The result was, however, that our strength, when weighted against that of our opponents, was weakness; and instead of gaining the object, we threw it at least half a century backwarder than it was when we began. The measure was popular, no doubt, among Dissenters, but unpopular with the irreligious.

My heart also revolts at all such plans and societies as are attended with parade. They do not appear to me to accord with the genius of that kingdom which cometh not with observation, or outward show; it was by a still, quiet, unostentatious process, that it was first obtained. The Pharisees demanded, when the kingdom of God should come? The answer of Jesus intimated that it would come without their seeing it, or being able to say where it was; nay, little as they might think of it, it was already amongst them.[9] Such appears to have been the process hitherto in the navy, and of the part that you have taken in it. One on board a ship is useful to another, and they to another, and so on. You found out individuals, and corresponded with them, and they brought you acquainted with others. On this principle, I should say, proceed. Find out suitable persons, one at each seaport, who would avail himself to ships coming in, to distribute tracts and bibles, which he would receive of the society, all in a still, prudent, unostentatious way, neither blowing a trumpet before him, nor sounding it abroad in magazines or newspapers when it was done. Keep an account of all your expenses, and if good be done, the public will know it and repay you. Correspond as much as you are able with the ships, and engage other evangelical ministers of different denominations to do the same. According to the number of ships which admit of correspondence, such should be the number of correspondents. Three or four in aid of you would be sufficient

---

[8] The Corporation and Test Acts had been passed in 1661 and 1673 respectively. The Corporation Act required, among other things, all magistrates, officers and members of municipal corporations to take an oath of allegiance to the crown and to affirm that in the preceding year they had received the Lord's Supper according to the rites of the Church of England. The Test Act, which was primarily aimed at Roman Catholics, required all officers who held civil or military posts to swear their allegiance to the crown, to partake of the Lord's Supper according to the rites of the established church and to deny the veracity of the Roman Catholic doctrine of transubstantiation. Both acts also discriminated against Dissenters, who sought to have them revoked in the late eighteenth century.

[9] See Luke 17:20–21.

at present. By this simple proceeding, it seems to me all the ends you propose might be answered, as well, if not better, than by the other; and this would be acting upon the principle which God hath already blessed.

A society on the plan you propose, seems to me an unwieldly, ostentatious affair, in which there would be great danger, at least, of miscarriage—of more attention being paid to the honour of the thing than to the thing itself—and of more time being taken up, and more money spent in adjustments, than in doing the work. You calculate upon the number of seamen, and the quantity of guilt and wretchedness among them, and wish for an institution that shall cover the whole at once. This is benevolent, but it is not God's usual way. When the world, after the flood, had all gone into idolatry, he could at once have met the tide, and turned it; but he called Abraham alone, and blessed him, and increased him, and said unto him, "I will bless thee, and thou shalt be a blessing."[10] The kingdom of heaven does not resemble the proposed siege of Hushai the Archite (a scheme not intended to succeed) in which all Israel were to bring ropes to the city, and draw it into the river, until there should not be one stone left upon another,[11] but is likened to a little leaven, hid in three measures of meal, till the whole was leavened.[12] I can see God's hand in what has been done hitherto; and I love to see it, rather than the hand of men.

It is one of Satan's devices, where he cannot quench the zeal of a servant of Christ, to turn it into a wrong direction. We have a missionary in the east, whose zeal was great, and I believe very disinterested; but he had nearly been overset by this device. He was exceedingly dissatisfied with having only a few hundred of the New Testament in the language of the natives to distribute around his station, pleading the many millions of souls who were perishing round him for lack of knowledge (as though all had stood ready to read, and all Christendom had nothing to but to furnish them with testaments) and unless he could meet the wants of all, he might as well do nothing. Thus, by aiming at things which are beyond reach, we may be in danger of neglecting those which are within reach.

After all, far be it from me to wish to govern you, or any of my brothers; I only show my opinion, and leave it. If you and others think it right to proceed on a different plan, do so; but I must be excused from having any concern in it. Indeed, I can only offer a little general advice upon any plan; for, partly owing to my inland situation, and partly to my numerous engagements in the Baptist Mission, it were impossible for me to carry on a new course of correspondence,

---

[10] Genesis 12:2.

[11] 2 Samuel 17:13.

[12] Matthew 13:33.

either by sea or land. Good Mr. Hitchings, of Stoke, I know very well.[13] I am sorry that Lieut. Marks should think of going to sea no more. He seems to have been a blessing indeed on board the *Conqueror*.[14] I will mention what you say of the interference of government having an unhappy effect on captains, though I do not suppose any interference will be made by governments as such, nor in any other way than gentle recommendation.

May God direct your way. I am, my dear brother, affectionately yours, A. Fuller.

---

[13] Otherwise unknown.

[14] The H.M.S. Conqueror had been built in 1800, saw action at the Battle of Trafalgar (1805), and was a ship of the line in the Royal Navy till 1821. See Robert Holden Mackenzie, *The Trafalgar Roll* (London: George Allen & Co., 1913), 147–150.

Richard Marks (1778–1847) was an enlisted seaman who rose through the ranks to become a master's mate on board the H.M.S. Defence, which also saw action at Trafalgar. His sterling conduct during that battle led to his promotion to lieutenant. In 1810 he left the Royal Navy to study theology at the University of Cambridge. He became curate of the Anglican parish at Waterbeach, Cambridgeshire, in 1812. Eight years later he was appointed vicar of Great Missenden, Buckinghamshire, where he served for 24 years. He was widely known for his robust Evangelical convictions, both during and after his service in the navy. See Blake, *Evangelicals in the Royal Navy*, 228–267.

"A juster idea of character": Robert Hall, Jr. on the competing biographies of Andrew Fuller by J.W. Morris and John Ryland, Jr

introd. and ed. C. Ryan Griffith

C. Ryan Griffith has a doctorate in Church History from The Southern Baptist Theological Seminary, where he wrote his thesis on John Ryland, Jr. He taught for a number of years at Bethlehem College and Seminary, before serving as the Executive Director of The Gospel Coalition.

In the July 1991 issue of *Baptist Quarterly*, Geoffery Nuttall briefly reviewed a fascinating collection of forty-one letters between Robert Hall, Jr. (1764–1831) and John Ryland, Jr. (1753–1825), then held by the Selly Oak College Library, Birmingham. The Hall–Ryland correspondence stretches from 1791–1824 and contains comments on funeral sermons and epitaphs for Robert Hall, Sr. (1728–1791) and Caleb Evans (1737–1791), expressions of shared concern for the health of fellow minister Andrew Fuller (1754–1815), notice of issues facing the Baptist Missionary Society and its missionaries, requests for pulpit supplies, revisions to sermon manuscripts, and counsel concerning a number of theological challenges facing Baptist congregations.[1] Some of this correspondence had been redacted and published in Olinthus Gregory's (1774–1841) *The*

---

[1] Geoffrey F. Nuttall, "Letters from Robert Hall to John Ryland 1791–1824," *The Baptist Quarterly* 34, no. 3 (July 1991): 127–131.

Works of Robert Hall, A.M. (1835).[2]

Among the most interesting items is a letter dated 25 October 1815, part of a collection of Hall's correspondence now housed at the University of Birmingham's Cadbury Research Library.[3] Hall's letter sheds light on the controversy surrounding the publication of two competing biographies on Hall and Ryland's recently departed friend, Andrew Fuller–one by printer and former pastor, J.W. Morris (1763–1836), and the other by John Ryland, himself.

The background

It was expected that Ryland, Fuller's closest living friend, would compile Fuller's memoir and oversee the publication of his works. Nine days before his death, Fuller wrote Ryland:

> We have enjoyed very much together, which I hope will prove an earnest of greater enjoyment in another world ... If I should never see your face in the flesh, I could wish one last testimony of brotherly love and of the truth of the gospel to be expressed, by your coming over, and preaching my funeral Sermon, if it can be, from Romans 8:10.[4]

It was the last letter Fuller dictated. Fuller died on May 7, 1815; he and Ryland had been friends for 37 years. In his funeral sermon for Fuller, Ryland remarked:

> After a longer and more intimate acquaintance than I have had with any other minister, there is no one to whom I could more confidently apply the emphatic phrase which the Apostle uses concerning himself, "I knew a man in Christ" (2 Cor 12:2)—a man whose temper and conduct, in a variety of private as well as public concerns, led me to consider him as not only a true believer in Christ, vitally united to him; but as one of the most conscientious, faithful, and spiritually minded men on earth; who might truly affirm, "For me to live is Christ."[5]

Ryland admitted that he "had no friend with whom I kept up so constant and

---

[2] See Robert Hall, *The Works of Robert Hall, A.M.*, ed. Olinthus Gregory, (London: Holdsworth and Ball, 1835), vol. 5.

[3] DA20/1/1 item 19, held at Cadbury Research Library: Special Collections, University of Birmingham.

[4] John Ryland, *The Indwelling and Righteousness of Christ No Security against Corporeal Death, but the Source of Spiritual and Eternal Life* (Kettering: J.G. Fuller, 1815), 35.

[5] Ryland, *Indwelling and Righteousness of Christ*, 2.

so profitable a correspondence."[6] Fuller's widow, Anne, soon wrote to Ryland, stating that there was "was no one better acquainted with the dear deceased in his public character, than yourself." While she forbade him from holding Fuller up "in the style of a panegyric," she expressed her certainty that her husband's memoirs "may be safely left" to Ryland's discretion.[7]

While Hall was also a close friend of Fuller and preached alongside Ryland at Fuller's funeral, he was confident that Ryland was the right choice for publishing his memoirs. A few days after Fuller's death, Hall wrote to Congregationalist Joseph Fletcher (1784–1843) minister of Stepney Meeting, "Dr. Ryland will, I believe, compile a pretty extensive memoir of him. He has been strongly urged to do so."[8] Ryland, apparently, began the work right away. He contacted Hall in June of 1815, requesting permission to publish Hall's funeral oration. Hall refused, noting that the "wretched oration" was the product of "extreme depression of spirits." He also discouraged Ryland from publishing the sermon Ryland had preached at Fuller's funeral, especially if Ryland planned to publish Fuller's memoirs. The sermons, he argued,

> are utterly unnecessary, if the memoirs are published; not only so, but they would stand in each other's way. When a biography is published, it is not, I think, usual for the same person to publish a funeral sermon previously. It is slaking the public curiosity prematurely. If you persist in your intention of publishing memoirs, I should feel no objection to taking opportunity of testifying my profound esteem and friendship for dear Mr. Fuller in some form which you may deem most eligible.[9]

Despite the challenges, Ryland completed Fuller's memoirs in the fall of 1815, sending the manuscript to Hall through Isaac James (1759–1828), a member of Ryland's Broadmead congregation.[10] Hall composed the letter transcribed below in October of the same year, returning with it Ryland's manuscript and giving his judgment on both Ryland's memoir and another, by J.W. Morris, which he had recently received.

While Morris had also been a close friend to Fuller and Ryland, their friendship had been deeply strained in the years leading up to Fuller's death. Origi-

---

[6] Ryland, *Indwelling and Righteousness of Christ*, 35.

[7] Andrew Fuller, *The Complete Works of the Rev. Andrew Fuller: With a Memoir of His Life*, ed. Andrew Gunton Fuller (Boston: Gould, Kendall and Lincoln, 1836), 1:94.

[8] Hall, *Works of Robert Hall*, 5:492.

[9] Hall, *Works of Robert Hall*, 5:494.

[10] See note 25 on Isaac James, below.

nally trained as a printer, Morris was called into ministry in his early twenties and was pastor of the Baptist congregation in Clipston from 1784 until 1803. While in Clipston, Morris started a printing house which soon printed the circular letters of the Northamptonshire Association and the *Periodical Accounts* of the Baptist Missionary Society—associations with which Morris was intimately involved. In 1801, Morris began publishing *The Biblical Magazine,* a bi-monthly (beginning in 1802, monthly) periodical of which he was editor, proprietor, and printer.[11] The magazine emerged in a crowded field of Christian publications and, despite its merger in 1804 with the Congregationalist *Theological Magazine and Review*, the newly retitled *Theological and Biblical Magazine* struggled to cover its costs. By 1809, Morris was forced to declare bankruptcy.[12] Typical of evangelical thought at the time, Fuller and Ryland found it untenable for Morris to continue in public ministry since his failure to manage his finances impinged upon his qualifications as an elder. Morris was forced to leave the Dunstable pastorate where he had moved in 1803 and never again pastored a church. Morris persisted in blaming his misfortune on the failure of others and refused to acknowledge the pride and intransigence which had put his business on shaky footing. Fuller wrote to Morris, pleading with him to confess his sin and be reconciled both to God and to his faithful friends. With repentance, Fuller promised, "the days of past friendship and affection" would be revived.[13] Morris, however, refused and his continued impenitence drove a bitter wedge between himself and Fuller, Ryland, and their fellow minister John Sutcliff (1752–1814). The breach in their friendship was never healed.

Thus, there is a hint of shock in Hall's letter. He seems surprised by Morris' presumption in preparing a memoir of Fuller for print, a task Hall and others saw properly falling to Ryland.[14] Morris, on the other hand, clearly saw himself as the rightful biographer. In the preface of his *Memoirs of the Life and Writings of the Rev. Andrew Fuller* (1816), Morris strongly defends his unequalled qualification for writing Fuller's memoir. In ornamented prose, Morris also

---

[11] Michael A.G. Haykin, *One Heart and One Soul: John Sutcliff of Olney, His Friends and His Times* (Darlington, Durham: Evangelical Press, 1994), 282.

[12] Haykin, *One Heart and One Soul*, 285.

[13] Quoted in Haykin, *One Heart and One Soul*, 286.

[14] A review of Morris' *Memoirs* in the October 1830 issue of the *American Baptist Magazine* noted: "The family of the departed immediately announced that arrangements were made, by which a Memoir would be given to the world by Mr. Fuller's most intimate friend, the Rev. Dr. Ryland of Bristol. This produced high expectations. But before the publication of this work could possibly take place, 'The Memoirs of the Life and Writings of the Rev. Andrew Fuller, late Pastor of the Baptist church at Kettering, &c. &c. By J. W. Morris,' appeared from the press" ("Review of J. W. Morris' 'Memoirs of the Life and Writings of the Rev. Andrew Fuller, Late Pastor of the Baptist Church at Kettering, and First Secretary to the Baptist Missionary Society,'" *The American Baptist Magazine* [October 1830], 303).

expresses his desire for Fuller's account to find its place among other notable examples of eighteenth-century biography.[15] Strikingly absent from his preface, particularly in contrast to Ryland's 1816 volume, is any mention of the proceeds from the sale of the biography going to Fuller's widow and children.[16] Given Morris' financial situation, profit from the volume's sale would have been a strong incentive for its urgent publication. Such a motive seemed apparent to William Carey (1761–1834) some years later. In a letter to his sisters in October of 1831, Carey expressed deep concern over Morris' eagerness to present Carey as a celebrity missionary:

> Dear Morris wrote to me for letters and other documents to assist him in writing memoirs of me after my death, but there was a spirit in his letter which I must disapprove. I therefore told him so in my reply, and absolutely refused to send anything. Indeed, I have no wish that anyone should write or say anything about me; let my memorial sleep with my body in the dust and at the last great day all the good or evil which belongs to my character will be fully known.[17]

By many accounts, Morris' edition of Fuller's biography was more successful than Ryland's.[18] Morris would go on to have a prolific career in writing and publishing. He published a second edition of Fuller's *Memoirs* in 1826, as well

---

[15] John Webster Morris, *Memoirs of the Life and Writings of the Rev. Andrew Fuller* (London: T. Hamilton, 1816), v–viii.

[16] Ryland wrote in his preface that he did not "hesitate to profess that I have undertaken this office, of giving a faithful representation of my dear departed Brother's life, not under the influence of any wish to display my skill as a writer of biography, nor yet to appear as a critic on his publications; but with the hope of promoting pure and undefiled religion, founded on truly evangelical principles and also with a desire of securing to the family of my beloved friend, the profits which may result from laying this sketch of his history before the public" (John Ryland, *The Work of Faith, the Labour of Love, and the Patience of Hope, Illustrated in the Life and Death of the Reverend Andrew Fuller: Late Pastor of the Baptist Church at Kettering, and Secretary to the Baptist Missionary Society, from Its Commencement, in 1792* [London: Button & Son, 1816], v).

[17] Earnest A. Payne, "A Carey Letter of 1831," *Baptist Quarterly* 9, no. 4 (October 1938): 240.

[18] Morris' description of Fuller's character was so elegant that it was frequently mentioned in literary reviews. See "Brief Sketches of Books: Memoirs of the Life and Writings of the Rev. Andrew Fuller. By J.W. Morris," *Magazine of the Dutch Reformed Church* (March 1827); also "Review of J. W. Morris' 'Memoirs of the Life and Writings of the Rev. Andrew Fuller,'" 303. In the 1884 edition of the *Complete Works of Andrew Fuller*, editor Joseph Belcher inserted a lengthy excerpt from Morris' biography near the end of Andrew Gunton Fuller's biographical memoir. Belcher wrote, "Perhaps this is a proper place to introduce a general view of Mr. Fuller's person, habits, and character, which I regret my valued brother [Andrew Gunton Fuller] has not incorporated into the memoir. No one knew Mr. Fuller better than his earliest biographer, the Rev. J.W. Morris" (Andrew Fuller, *The Complete Works of the Rev. Andrew Fuller: With a Memoir of His Life*, ed. Joseph Belcher [Philadelphia, PA: American Baptist Publication Society, 1884], 1:105).

as a compendious collection of Fuller's writings in the same year. Morris published a two-volume *History of the Christian Church from the Apostolic Age to the Times of Wycliffe the Reformer* (1827), and edited both an abridgment of William Gurnall's (1616–1679) *Spiritual Warfare* and *The Complete Works of Robert Hall* in 1828. By 1833, he had completed *Biographical Recollections of the Rev. Robert Hall, A.M.* and his own *Sacred Biography, forming a Connected History of the Old and New Testament*.[19] Morris' output was significant and by the end of his life it seems that he had overcome the financial troubles that dogged the first decade of his career.

The letter
Shortly after Hall's death in 1831, Olinthus Gregory, a mathematical master at the Royal Military Academy at Woolwich, oversaw the collection and publication of Hall's works. Gregory had come to know Hall in the late 1790s when he was a member of Hall's St. Andrews Street Baptist Church in Cambridge. Gregory's ambition to publish Hall's works appears to be grounded in his deep admiration for Hall's piety and preaching and dates back at least to November 1799, when Hall allowed Gregory to "follow him wherever he went, to obtain 'copy' as it should be needed."[20] Gregory included the letter from Hall to Ryland in volume five of *The Works of Robert Hall, A.M.* (1835), but with several significant editorial changes.[21] First, Gregory removed three sentences that shed light on Hall's overall assessment of Ryland's historical work. In them, Hall expresses that he finds little need for alteration of Ryland's manuscript and that Ryland's account appears to him as being "sufficiently correct." In Hall's estimation, Ryland's biography "will give much satisfaction to the friends of our invaluable deceased Brother, as well as to the religious public at large."

Gregory also expunged Hall's specific reference to J.W. Morris as the author of the nearly-completed biography of which he "highly disapproved." Hall wrote that he "need scarcely say that I absolutely declined" to endorse Morris' work, "informing him it was impossible for me to do it without a violation of honor and consistency." Hall also expressed his disappointment over Morris' distorted treatment of Fuller, particularly his tendency to magnify Fuller's

---

[19] William Perkins, "Morris, John Webster," ed. Sidney Lee, *Dictionary of National Biography, 1885–1900* (London: Elder Smith & Co., 1894), s.v.

[20] Hall, *Works of Robert Hall*, 1:11.

[21] Hall, *Works of Robert Hall*, 5:499–500.

faults. He gently chided Ryland for his tendency towards the opposite. Nonetheless, Hall conceded that "it is not impossible that posterity may obtain a juster idea of the character of our excellent friend by comparing them than by either of them separately."

Finally, the Gregory publication removed the letter's final paragraph in which Hall advised Ryland on the timing of a collected edition of Fuller's works. Hall argued that delaying the publication of Fuller's works would meet with greater success. While immediate publication might be a source of income for Fuller's widow, Hall suggested that the Baptist Missionary Society might provide Fuller's pension to his widow rather than "hawking" Fuller's writings. Ryland would heed this advice, issuing Fuller's collected works nearly a decade later. [22]

It is not altogether clear as to why Gregory made these changes. The most compelling possibility is that Gregory removed specific references as a courtesy to Morris, who was still living when Hall's *Works* were published. By the 1830s, Morris was an established—even successful—author, having simply outlived the earlier criticisms of Ryland and Fuller.

The complete letter thus provides several valuable insights into the circumstances surrounding Ryland and Morris' 1816 biographies. It gives us an early assessment of the competing biographies of Fuller and how his legacy was being evaluated. It also gives evidence that Morris' biography was not warmly received by Hall, one of Fuller's closest friends. Almost definitely this was the result of Morris' refusal to repent and be reconciled to ministers in the Northamptonshire Association. Hall may well have seen less spiritual value in Morris' approach and his characterization of Fuller. Hall also probably took umbrage at Morris' presumption to publish Fuller's *Memoir* in the first place. Nevertheless, the letter also demonstrates a charity and hopefulness that was common to evangelicals of the Fuller circle—even if the Morris biography was ill-intentioned, unflattering, and inconveniently timed. Hall recognized that the publication of both accounts would providentially give an even "juster idea of the character of our most excellent friend."

---

[22] See his eight-volume edition of Andrew Fuller, *The Works of the Rev. Andrew Fuller, Late of Kettering, Northamptonshire* (London: B.J. Holdsworth, 1824).

Letter from Rev. Robert Hall, Jr. to John Ryland, Jr.[23]

[October 25, 1815][24]

My dear Sir,

I have availed myself of the opportunity of returning your manuscript by M[r] James.[25] I am much pleased with it as far as it has proceeded, and judging from this specimen have no doubt it will give much satisfaction to the friends of our invaluable deceased Brother, as well as to the religious public at large.

In page 1 of the first letter of M[r] Fuller I have inserted interesting and useful instead of agreeable. I have also here and there inserted a word in other parts of the manuscript, but found little room for alteration. It appears to me sufficiently correct.[26] I found the whole narrative respecting his child & his first wife exceedingly affecting & interesting. I think you have done right in relating it as it puts his domestic character in a most interesting light. It shows how perfectly compatible is great tenderness of heart and an attention to minuter duties with great powers of intellect and an ardent pursuit of great objects. Biographers have been usually too sparing of such details. How delighted should we have been with such an exhibition of the church of

---

[23] This letter is located in "Correspondence of Robert Hall to John Ryland, Jr." DA20/1/1/19 (Special Collections, Cadbury Research Library. University of Birmingham, UK). My thanks to Dr. Timothy Whelan who provided valuable feedback on the transcription of this letter.

[24] An edited form of this letter was published in *Works of Robert Hall*, 5:548–551.

[25] Isaac James (1759–1828) of Bristol. James was married to Jane Hall (d. 1834), daughter of Robert Hall (1728–1791), on April 20, 1789. James was educated at the Baptist College at Bristol, but at the end of his term he became concerned that the Lord had not called him into pastoral ministry. He studied medicine in London for several years before returning to his birthplace in Hitchin to open an academy. When his maternal uncle, John Needham of Bristol, died, James returned to Bristol and became classical tutor at the Academy, where he served alongside Ryland for 30 years (S.J.B., "A Brief Biographical Notice of Mr. Isaac James, of Bristol," *The Christian's Penny Magazine* 123 [October 11, 1834]: 326–328). Robert Hall mentioned James as part of the Broadmead congregation at Bristol (Letter LXXVII to Arthur Tozer. August 11, 1825 [*Works of Robert Hall*, 5:548–551]. In early letters to Tozer (a deacon at Broadmead) Hall asked the recipient to greet Mr. James and "my sisters," but by October 3, 1825, he wrote: "Greet Mr. and Mrs. James and my sister" (Letter LXXVIII to Arthur Tozer [*Works of Robert Hall*, 5:551–553]. The latter he later identifies as Mary (Letter LXXIX to Arthur Tozer, December 6, 1825 [*Works of Robert Hall*, 5:555]. Mary was part of Broadmead and remained unmarried until her death in 1843 at the age of 86 (Robert Hall Warren, *The Hall Family* [Bristol: J. W. Arrowsmith, 1910], 33).

[26] The first three sentences of this paragraph do not appear in Gregory's transcription in *Works of Robert Hall*, vol. 5.

Edwards & Howe & other illustrious Christian heroes.[27]

Morris has wrote to M[r] Broughton[28] earnestly importuning me to review his *Life of Mr Fuller* which is completed to the last chapter. I need scarcely say that I absolutely declined, informing him it was impossible for me to do it without a violation of honor and consistency. I suppose his book which is to be a 12[s] will be out shortly.[29] I hope and believe however it will not prevent your work from obtaining a considerable circulation. Though I highly disapprove of Morris's publication, it is not impossible that posterity may obtain a juster idea of the character of our excellent friend by comparing them than by either of them separately. I am afraid my dear Brother will be as sparing of his shades as M of his lights. Though his faults were trivial indeed compared to his excellencies, yet they were in my view very apparent, and as is generally the case in very forcible characters, they possessed a certain prominence. On the whole however it will be long before we look on ~~another~~ such a man.

With respect to the republication of his works, I think it would be much better to defer it for some years. Most of them are at present in the possession of the religious public in a separate form, and therefore will not be much disposed to

---

[27] The writings of New Haven Congregationalist Jonathan Edwards (1703–1758) were well known to both Hall and Ryland. Hall began reading Edwards in his childhood, having "perused and reperused" his works by age nine (Hall, *The Works of Robert Hall*, 1:5). Presumably, Hall was acquainted with Samuel Hopkins' (1721–1803) biography of Edwards, but judged it insufficiently detailed. Ryland had read the Boston edition (1765) as early as 1773. On a pastedown inside the front cover of his father's copy, Ryland inscribed "the life of the greatest, wisest, and humblest, & holyest of uninspired men."

Puritan John Howe (1630–1705) served as curate at Great Torrington, Devonshire, beginning in 1654. In 1656, he traveled to London to serve as chaplain to Oliver Cromwell (1599–1658) in Whitehall. After the fall of Richard Cromwell (1626–1712), he returned to his congregation in Devon. With the 1662 Act of Uniformity, Howe withdrew from the Church of England and became a Nonconformist. Hall wrote that he had learned far more from Howe "than from any other author I have ever read. There is an astonishing magnificence in his conceptions" (Hall, *The Works of Robert Hall*, 1:163). Hall exhorted a fellow minister to read "the wonderful Howe" for his practical and experimental divinity, of which he considered Howe's *Living Temple* and *Treatise on Delighting in God* as being the best representatives (Hall, *The Works of Robert Hal*, 1:303). Historian Edmund Calamy (1671–1732), grandson of the Puritan divine Edmund Calamy (1600–1666), published a memoir of the life of Howe in London in 1724. Apparently, Hall considered this volume, also, as too "sparing" in detail.

[28] Samuel Broughton (1787–1837) of Spading, Lincolnshire. Samuel Broughton was the son of Rev. Thomas Broughton (1704–1774), M.A., rector of St Peter's, Bristol. Samuel was appointed an army surgeon in 1812 and served in the south of France until the end of the Napoleonic wars. Broughton was later a prominent physician in London and elected as a fellow of the Royal Society and of the Geological Society (Leslie Stephen, ed. *Dictionary of National Biography* [London: Smith, Elder, & Co, 1886], 6:403). It appears that J.W. Morris sent his narrative of Fuller's life to his son, Jesse Morris (died 1828) in hopes of using Broughton to secure a review from Robert Hall. Jesse had begun working for Samuel Broughton in 1814. See *The New Baptist Miscellany* 2 [1828]: 309-310 for the obituary entry for Jesse [J.T] Morris, the third son of J.W. Morris, who died on June 25, 1828 at the age of 36. Apparently, J.W. Morris lost three sons "in the prime of life."

[29] 12[s] is presumably "twelve shillings."

pay 4 or 5 guineas for them again. After 12 or 15 years they might be collected & published to great advantage; in the mean time, it would be easy for the Society to provide for M.^{rs} F by a note similar to the last renewed from year to year. This would be more honorable to Mr F. than to be hawking his publications & pressing them on the public for the avowed purpose of providing for his family. With kind rememb.^{es} to Mrs R. & your family as well as all friends. I I remain dear Sr ever yours. R. Hall.[30]

---

[30] This final paragraph does not appear in the transcription in *Works of Robert Hall*, vol. 5.

Book Reviews

*The Puritan Experiment: Papers read at the
2019 Westminster Conference*
(The Westminster Conference, 2019), 128 pages.
Available from: John Harris, 18 Nook Green,
Dewsbury, West Yorkshire WF12 0BJ.

Founded by Martyn Lloyd-Jones (1899–1981) and J.I. Packer (1926–2020), the Westminster Conference (formerly the Puritan Conference) has provided rich and robust evangelical and reformed reflections on theology and church history for over seventy-five years or so. The conference is held over the course of two days, normally in December, with three papers being delivered each day and with each of the addresses followed by vigorous discussion. The six papers given at the 2019 conference dealt with various aspects of the "Puritan Experiment." Three of them dealt largely with thematic subjects—those by Jeremy Walker (on the principle of Puritan worship), Robert Strivens (on the practice of Puritan worship), and Matthew Bingham (on the emergence of Independency)—and three with Puritan prosopography—Joseph Pipa (on William Perkins), Douglas McCallum (on Thomas Manton), and Paul Smith (on the Pilgrim Fathers).

Given that the majority of those attending the conference are in pastoral leadership, the papers are normally designed to not only inform the mind, but also to recover key elements of the Christian past for the modern day. After outlining the actual practice of Puritan worship, for instance, Strivens asks a series of penetrating questions regarding how Puritan practice might inform worship today (p.62–63). Again, after detailing the life of Pekins and his historical context, Joseph Pipa's study of William Perkins points to three lessons from Perkins' life for the modern preacher (p.28).

From an historian's point of view, the one essay that I found particularly fascinating was that of Matthew Bingham, who teaches at Oak Hill College. Bingham looks at four factors in the emergence of the English Independents —the precedent of previous separatist movements (he identifies Henry Jacob (1563–1624) as being critical here [p.70–71]), persecution, geography, and the impact of print culture in the 1640s—and then draws three lessons for their modern descendants (p.81–84). In his "Applicatory Conclusion" Bingham notes that the first person to use the term "Congregational Way" in print was actually the Particular Baptist William Kiffen (1616–1701), whose ecclesial journey typifies the importance placed by the Independents on ecclesiology (p.83–84). Possibly the last time that Kiffen's name has been mentioned in this conference was in 1978, when Lloyd-Jones Martyn Lloyd-Jones delivered his final paper to the conference on "John Bunyan: Church Union" (see *Light from John Bunyan and Other Puritans* [The Westminster Conference, 1978], 96–97), and criticized Kiffen for his rigidity in his debate with Bunyan over open and closed communion. So, it was good to see Kiffen cited positively and an important lesson drawn from his ecclesial convictions.

Michael A.G. Haykin
The Southern Baptist Theological Seminary.

David Horspool, *Oliver Cromwell: England's Protector*
([London]: Allen Lane, 2017), viii+132 pages.

While there have been no shortage of Cromwell biographies over the years, this one by David Horspool, the History editor of the *Times Literary Supplement*, is most welcome, since, as Horspool puts it, "Cromwell's life has not been written about in full for a surprisingly long time" (p.119). At 110 pages or so, Horspool's biography is not, of course, a full study of the quintessential Puritan soldier and statesman. Yet, it touches on all of the key aspects of Cromwell's career in a fresh and eminently readable manner: his remarkable rise to power and time as a soldier in the field, and his profoundly important religious convictions and troubled rule of England in the 1650s. His disputed legacy, however—he was essentially loathed by many till his rehabilitation by the Victorians—is only lightly touched on (p.110–111).

Horspool rightly notes that of "all the momentous issues that concentrated his mind" during his life, "religion remained his principal concern." Of course, he was not unique in this: for most seventeenth-century men and women, "religion was not a part of life, but the point of it" (p.21). But unless this key to understanding Cromwell is taken as a hermeneutical principle, it is very hard for secular-minded twenty-first-century readers to make sense of this larger-than-life Puritan. Although Cromwell never formally belonged to any church membership, he was definitely partial to Independency, or Congregationalism, as it later came to be called, which brought him into conflict with the other major Puritan body, namely, the Presbyterians (p.40, 48). Like all of his Puritan contemporaries, though, Cromwell was a biblicist, for whom "Bible-reading was a cornerstone of worship" (p.41).

Alongside this biblicism, Cromwell's faith is well captured by a quote from a letter that he wrote to his brother-in-law, Valentine Walton, after the Battle of Marston Moor (July 2, 1644), when the Parliamentary forces utterly routed the troops loyal to the monarch, Charles I. Parliament had lost some three hundred men as opposed to over 4,100 Royalists killed. But among the Parliamentary dead was Cromwell's nephew, Valentine's son. Cromwell explained how he had died and then added, "the Lord took him into the happiness we all pant after and live for" (p.42). This consolatory remark opens up an entire window into what made Cromwell tick and what he lived for. Of course, there were blunders in his career: the most damaging of which occurred in the Irish campaign and the pitiless massacres at Drogheda and Wexford (p.83–87). Driving Cromwell was a "visceral hatred of the Catholic Irish," which was de rigueur for far too many Puritans (p.85).

Since the rise of democracy in the British Isles, it has been a given to trace its origins to Enlightenment authors like John Locke (who was a student at Oxford under Cromwell's one-time chaplain, John Owen). Yet Cromwell himself, after the decisive Battle of Naseby (June 14, 1645), which effectively ended the First English Civil War, could tell Parliament that the whole of the civil war could be boiled down to a fight for liberty of conscience (p.53). To be sure, Cromwell did not favour the principle of "one man one vote", which was famously enunciated by Thomas Rainsborough during the Putney Debates when he told Cromwell's son-in-law, Henry Ireton,

> the poorest he that is in England hath a life to live, as the greatest he; and therefore truly, sir, I think it's clear, that every man that is to live under a government ought first by his own consent to put himself under that government; and I do think that the poorest man in England is not at all bound in a strict sense to that government that he hath not had a voice to put himself under (p.69).

Yet, there seems little doubt that Cromwell wanted a regime where there was much greater freedom for religious dissent that than had hitherto been possible, and thus ironically, in this way, he played a role in the development of Anglophone democracy.

When he was in power, Cromwell was accused of hypocrisy and political deviousness (p.57, 76–77). But Horspool rejects this reading of his character. What some took to be deviousness, was actually Cromwell dithering—"Cromwell actually seems to have been a champion ditherer" (p.76)—seeking to know God's will. Securing victory on the battlefield—Cromwell never lost a major engagement in which he was involved and he naïvely took such victories as a sign of God's favour—turned out to be much easier than governing the nation amid the deep, and often personal, disagreements of his fellow Puritan victors.

Michael A.G. Haykin
The Southern Baptist Theological Seminary.

Rhys S. Bezzant, *Edwards the Mentor*
(New York: Oxford University Press, 2019); viii+208 pages.

Rhys S. Bezzant's book, *Edwards the Mentor*, is a philosophical treatise on mentoring much more than it is a historical treatment of Edwards. Bezzant provides a visual illustration of how mentorship has been done well historically through the lens of Jonathan Edwards. Since Bezzant incorporates a broad framework of people and ideas on mentoring, this work should be consulted when researching significant figures from this era to better understand the effects of others upon them. For example, while Andrew Fuller is not named in this volume, he is nevertheless from the same time-period as Edwards. Fuller not only enjoyed the writings of Edwards but is himself a product of mentoring. As a young man, and newly converted, Fuller developed a cherished spiritual friendship with Joseph Diver.

Bezzant's subject is fresh even though the secondary Edwardsean marketplace is oversaturated. His topic of mentorship is a needed new angle, which bridges an often-under-considered dichotomy between Edwards' public and private life. Edwards' pupils report in their diaries that the private Edwards was very friendly. This portrayal bucks against the reclusive and highly introverted often associated with Edwards. Edwards sought to move pulpit theology from the theoretical to the practical, so this angle is consistent as it is historically substantiated. Through four insightful chapters *Edwards the Mentor* demonstrates how Edwards's use of the time-tested mimetic praxis produced seismic changes throughout New England.

In the first chapter, the practice of mentoring as an ancient practice is considered as a means to nurture virtue within an individual. Two classical approaches to education are considered: *arete* and *mimesis*. Bezzant notes that the pursuit of excellence (*arete*) in isolation often produced stoic self-referential personalities. *Mimesis*, however, became a balancing approach proving to be necessary in the leadership of others. To this point, Edwards is seen as early-on devolving towards a hyper-introversion. Surprisingly, as if out of nowhere, Edwards stumbles upon *mimesis* during his first pastorate in New York. The older Mr. Smith provided for Edwards a mentorship model, which may have been lacking in his own life, and seems to have been replicated by Edwards with younger men in ministry.

To this point, Bezzant pieces together the traces of manuscript evidence from several of Edwards' mentees: Joseph Bellamy, Deborah Hatheway, Job Strong, Samuel Hopkins, and David Brainerd. In a chapter entitled "The Affective Turn," mentoring is seen to become a resource for parentless young people in an increasingly mobile age. Friṛ̣endship, or "the affective turn," increasingly became a place of self-discovery and self-disclosure during the eighteenth century. *In loco parentis* became for Edwards a way of assisting the Log College era of transition from adolescence to adulthood. Further, Edwards' "union of all things" theology was easily transferable to mentorship—even to the point of becoming family. Bellamy, Hopkins and Brainerd hold significant prominence in Edwards' ever-widening circle of relationships. While Hopkins was unsuccessful in wedding himself permanently into Edwards's family, Brainerd has the honor of being buried next to one of his daughters.

In the third chapter, Bezzant develops Edwards' theology of imitation. Edwards's use of *imago dei*, *imitatio Christi*, and the *visio dei* is seen to be the bones upon which the meat of his mimetic theology hangs. Narrative identity, as a means of relating Edwards' approach, shows how the beatific vision of God is the goal to which Edwards' life and vision sails. So, the story of Edwards' theology starts with creation. Out of creation comes the desire for communication as image-bearers with God himself. Life moves and flows *coram deo*. When a new spiritual sense is communicated to man, he is then able to imitate the True Man. This reshaping occurs through imitation and moves toward the goal of union by a beatific vision of God.

The final chapter presents the mentoring legacy of Edwards through the experience of his son during the American Revolution era. Regrettably, most biography of Edwards Jr. is accented by the Romanticism pendulum swing away from the Enlightenment era of Edwards' son. Happily, Bezzant pays recognition to the influence that Edwards' mentees had on the orphaned son of Edwards. Edwards Jr.'s mid-twentieth century biographers tend to accent his apparent distance from his father's theology. However, more recent scholarship is beginning to realign the received narrative, to which is further evidence that Edwards Sr.'s mentoring legacy is even more impressive.

Perhaps one of the most surprising and relevant aspects of Bezzant's book is his concluding *Coda*. The *Coda* highlights the potential for our virtual world of social media to be chaotic and potentially short-circuiting mentorship. The *Coda* instructs us to reconsider face-to-face mentorship. While unstated by Bezzant, the reader is left to consider what kinds of mentoring have been the most helpful in his or her own life, and furthermore, what practical changes could be made to increase the potential good in that of others. As a recommendation, this book is not only for Edwards or Andrew Fuller scholars, but also for professors and pastors who need to revise what successful mentorship looks like. Sadly, the price-point will keep this book out of the hands of most pastors, but perhaps in time, Bezzant will consider a popular-level resource based on this eminently helpful book.

John S. Banks, ThM studies,
The Southern Baptist Theological Seminary.

Richard T. Pollard, *Dan Taylor (1738–1816), Baptist Leader and Pioneering Evangelical*, Monographs in Baptist History, vol. 9 (Eugene, OR: Pickwick Publications, 2018), xiv+333 pages.

There are two main historic streams of English Baptist life: that of the General Baptists, the older of the two streams with its roots in the Elizabethan Separatist movement, and that of the Particular Baptists, which came out of the seventeenth-century London Puritan Jacob-Lathrop-Jessey church. The latter was the more numerous and progenitor of the majority of the English-speaking Baptist churches in the transatlantic Anglophone world. Most of the congregations of the former stream did not survive beyond the eighteenth century as they embraced various forms of serious heterodoxy. A renewal movement, though, did manage to perpetuate the General Baptist cause, under the denominational label of the New Connexion of General Baptists. At the fountainhead of this Baptist body was Dan Taylor (1738–1816), whose evangelical thought is the subject of this theological biography by Richard Pollard, the senior minister of Fishponds Baptist Church, Bristol.

While there is a major study that deals with Taylor's life, that of Frank Rinaldi (p.6–7), Pollard notes the lack of scholarly attention to Taylor's thought (p.5–8), and therefore the pressing need for this work. It bears recalling that Andrew Fuller, who tussled with Taylor in the 1780s over the issue of the extent of the atonement among other matters, regarded Taylor as an "invincible opponent" (p.141–178; quote from p.1). Taylor was first exposed to evangelical Christianity through the notable ministry of William Grimshaw of Haworth. His embrace of Evangelicalism was an adherence to a theological position that has been defined by historian David Bebbington as a perspective marked by biblicism, crucicentrism, conversionism, and activism (p.19–49).

Pollard then examines Taylor's defence of his soteriological views over against Arianism and Socinianism (p.65–104). It is noteworthy that there is no evidence that Taylor denied the perseverance of the saints and also that he fused Hugo Grotius' governmental theory of the death of Christ with a penal view of the atonement (p.76–86). Pollard argues that it is conceivable that the latter influenced Fuller's view of Christ's death (p.84). In 1788 Taylor accepted an invite to the home of Joseph Priestley. Their meeting was a cordial one and Taylor does not appear to have critiqued the man who was the leading apostle of Socinianism. Pollard sees this as a mark of Taylor's Evangelicalism: his "willingness to place respect above doctrinal disagreement was a further notable feature of his evangelicalism" (p.99; see also p.200).

Chapter 3 is focused on Taylor's commitment to the doctrine of general redemption, which he considered "the most glorious display of the Father's love" (p.105–140; quote from p.111). Taylor inherited some of his convictions in this regard from his early involvement in the Methodist movement. His views were sharpened by a response to a Particular Baptist text, namely, Robert Hall, Sr.'s *Help to Zion's Travellers*, a minor spiritual classic (p.112–113, 132). The next chapter deals with what Pollard rightly views as Taylor's most significant theological engagement, his quarrel with Andrew Fuller (p.141–178). Pollard views the irenicism that pervades their debate as typical of eighteenth-century Evangelicalism (p.144, 149–150). Yet, as the debate between John Wesley and Calvinists like Augustus Toplady in the "Zanchy affair" reveals, eighteenth-century Evangelicalism was not without its brutal side. Fuller's refusal to engage in *ad hominem* attacks may well be a key reason for the civility of the debate between him and Taylor.

Pollard argues convincingly, though, that Taylor's defence of general redemption played an enormous role in persuading Fuller to shift his view of the cross. From a commercial view of the atonement where Christ's death was for the exact number of the elect's sins, Fuller came to view his Lord's death as sufficient for all but efficacious for the elect (p.158–166). In this regard Taylor had a "commanding influence on Fuller" (p.178). The influence was not all one direction, though, as Pollard shows the ways that Fuller influenced Taylor, especially with regard to the sovereignty of God.

Taylor's ecclesiology is treated in Chapter 5 ("The Baptist Wesley," p.179–216) and his sacramental theology in Chapter 6 ("Creative Proponent," p.217–260). Taylor's commitment to hymn-singing is also treated in the latter (p.246–259). A final chapter looks at Taylor the "religious entrepreneur" (p.261–295), where Pollard discusses, among other things, Taylor's use of tracts (p.263–266), his commitment to church planting (p.268–272), and his willingness to work with men who did not share his soteriological distinctives, namely the Particular Baptists and Independents, for the sake of mission (p.278–284). The latter reflects the catholicity of eighteenth-century Evangelicalism, a spirit quite different from the "party spirit" of the Puritan era (p.282), which Pollard sees as supportive of Bebbington's argument of the clear difference between Evangelicals of the eighteenth century and their Puritan forebears (p.302–303). Pollard further suggests that the refusal to recognize the truth of Bebbington's argument stems in part from a reluctance to see the place of Arminianism in the emergence of Evangelicalism, which, in turn might explain why a prominent figure like Taylor has been overlooked (p.303–304).

All in all, this is an important and stimulating study that engages with both the details of Taylor's theology as well as larger implications of his place in church history. Highly recommended!

Michael A.G. Haykin
The Southern Baptist Theological Seminary.

Andrew Fuller, *The Complete Works of Andrew Fuller*,
Vol. IV: *Memoirs of the Rev. Samuel Pearce*,
ed. Michael A.G. Haykin (Berlin/Boston:
Walter de Gruyter GmbH, 2017), xvi+151 pages.

William Jay (1769-1853) once remarked about Samuel Pearce, "when I have endeavoured to form an image our Lord as a preacher, Pearce has oftener presented himself to my mind than any I have been acquainted with." This was high praise indeed considering that Jay had warm friendships with the likes of John Newton, Robert Hall, Rowland Hill and John Ryland. So, it is no surprise that Andrew Fuller desired to capture the life of the venerated preacher in his *Memoirs of the Rev. Samuel Pearce*.

This edition is the fourth volume in the new The *Complete Works of Andrew Fuller*, published by De Gruyter. Among his writings, perhaps only *The Gospel Worthy of All Acceptation* ranks higher than Fuller's memoir of Samuel Pearce. The book was very popular throughout the nineteenth century. And the reasons why are very apparent in Fuller's account of his friend. The biography reads as well today as it did when it was originally published.

Samuel Pearce (1766–1799) was the pastor of the Cannon Street Baptist Chapel in Birmingham, England. He was celebrated for his exemplary preaching. Few could match his pathos for the exaltation of Jesus Christ. But he was most noted for his tireless support of Baptist foreign missions. At one point he had designs to be a missionary to India, but his friends counseled him to remain in Britain as he would serve the cause better by raising support. As he was contemplating his decision, he kept a private journal. Fuller reproduces excerpts of the diary that reveal the heart of a man who desired to see the gospel preached in the unreached places. Pearce consistently resolved his soul to the disposal of the Lord so that God might be glorified among those who did not know him. He taught himself Bengali, writing, "the thought of exalting the redeemer in this language is a spur to my application paramount to every discouragement for want of a living tutor" (p.68). Fuller confessed that after reading the journal, even his friends wondered if they had made a mistake in requesting that he remain at home. In addition, the biography contains correspondence between Pearce's friends that demonstrate his pastoral heart. There are letters to church members, fellow pastors, missionaries and even those who were struggling with their faith (p.136). Pearce was passionate about the Bible, passionate about missions, passionate about souls and most of all passionate about his Savior.

With such a remarkable character, it is difficult to conceive that the *Memoir* could be improved. But the editor, Michael Haykin, has succeeded in doing so. He begins the volume with an introductory essay upon Pearce revealing some of the missing details surrounding the pastor's life. But he also assesses the reasons why Fuller undertook the project in the first place. Typical of the period, the proceeds of the book would benefit Pearce's widow and children. No doubt the well-being of his friend's family was foremost in his friend's mind as he wrote the biography. But Fuller also recognized that Pearce could be another David Brainerd—a person of exemplary character that would stimulate others toward missions (p.25–26). Fuller's prediction turned out to be correct. Pearce's life inspired generations of future missionaries and their supporters. But Haykin aptly notes the polemic nature of Fuller's memoir. In contrast to the adversaries (such a William Huntington and John Bradford) of what came to be known as "Fullerism," Pearce portrayed the best features of Fuller's theology. Much of his "ideas of preaching human obligation" feature in the conclusion of the biography (p.125). So, while the subject of the *Memoir* is Samuel Pearce, Haykin has appropriately assessed the work in light of Fuller's broader writings.

But the best attribute of this new edition is Michael Haykin's annotations to the text. Haykin demonstrates the variation in words, spellings and omissions between the six different volumes that were edited by the author during his lifetime. It allows the reader to see the change in Fuller's thinking and style as his writing evolved. But of primary importance is that Haykin brings his wealth of scholarship to illuminate the background of the subject. He provides brief biographical information for each character that is introduced in the *Memoir* including further literary references. He includes the origination of quotations from hymns and the Bible. There are notes on obscure facts such as a quote (see p.48) from the poet Robert Blair (1699–1746) to a passing reference of Francesco Spiera (1502–1548) who was a Protestant who denied his convictions when facing the Spanish Inquisition (p.72). Pearce remarked that he longed "to preach the gospel to the Booteas." Haykin was able to discover that this referred to the Bhutia, a Tibetan people group that migrated to North West Bengal (p.64). The scope of Haykin's knowledge on the subject is staggering. His research truly deepens the reader's understanding of the Birmingham pastor and his times. This volume is the new standard of Andrew Fuller's *Memoir of the Rev. Samuel Pearce.*

S. Blair Waddell
Senior Pastor, Providence Baptist Church,
Huntsville, Alabama.

CENTER for BAPTIST STUDIES
at THE SOUTHERN BAPTIST THEOLOGICAL SEMINARY

The Andrew Fuller Center for Baptist Studies, located at The Southern Baptist Theological Seminary in Louisville, Kentucky, seeks to promote the study of Baptist history as well as theological reflection on the contemporary significance of that history. The center is named in honor of Andrew Fuller (1754–1815), the late eighteenth- and early nineteenth- century English Baptist pastor and theologian, who played a key role in opposing aberrant thought in his day as well as being instrumental in the founding and early years of the Baptist Missionary Society. Fuller was a close friend and theological mentor of William Carey, one of the pioneers of that society.

The Andrew Fuller Center holds an annual two-day conference in September that examines various aspects of Baptist history and thought. It also supports the publication of the critical edition of the Works of Andrew Fuller, and from time to time, other works in Baptist history. The Center seeks to play a role in the mentoring of junior scholars interested in studying Baptist history.

andrewfullercenter.org

# DE GRUYTER

The Andrew Fuller Works Project

It is with deep gratitude to God that The Andrew Fuller Center for Baptist Studies announces that the publishing house of Walter de Gruyter, with head offices in Berlin and Boston, has committed itself to the publication of a modern critical edition of the entire corpus of Andrew Fuller's published and unpublished works. Walter de Gruyter has been synonymous with high-quality, landmark publications in both the humanities and sciences for more than 260 years. The preparation of a critical edition of Fuller's works, part of the work of the Andrew Fuller Center, was first envisioned in 2004. It is expected that this edition will comprise twelve to fourteen volumes and take seven or so years to publish.

The importance of the project

The controlling objective of The Works of Andrew Fuller Project is to preserve and accurately transmit the text of Fuller's writings. The editors are committed to the finest scholarly standards for textual transcription, editing, and annotation. Transmitting these texts is a vital task since Fuller's writings, not only for their volume, extent, and scope, but for their enduring importance, are major documents in both the Baptist story and the larger history of British Dissent.

From a merely human perspective, if Fuller's theological works had not been written, William Carey would not have gone to India. Fuller's theology was the mainspring behind the formation and early development of the Baptist Missionary Society, the first foreign missionary society created by the Evangelical Revival of the last half of the eighteenth century and the missionary society under whose auspices Carey went to India. Very soon, other missionary societies were established, and a new era in missions had begun as the Christian faith was increasingly spread outside of the West, to the regions of Africa and Asia. Carey was most visible at the fountainhead of this movement. Fuller, though not so visible, was utterly vital to its genesis.

andrewfullercenter.org/the-andrew-fuller-works-project

H&E Publishing is a Canadian evangelical publishing company located out of Peterborough, Ontario. We exist to provide Christ-exalting, Gospel-centred, and Bible-saturated content aimed to show God to be as glorious and worthy as He truly is.

hesedandemet.com

www.ingramcontent.com/pod-product-compliance
Lightning Source LLC
Chambersburg PA
CBHW021429070526
44577CB00001B/133